PREACHING FOR A RESPONSE

R. Warren Lathem
Dan W. Dunn

Preaching for a Response

Published by Bristol House, Ltd.

First Printing, June 2008

ISBN: 978-1-885224-65-1
Printed in the United States of America.

BRISTOL HOUSE, LTD.
1201 E. 5th St., Suite 2107
Anderson, Indiana 46012
Phone: 765-644-0856
Fax: 765-622-1045

To order call: 1-800-451-READ (7323)
www.bristolhouseltd.com

TABLE OF CONTENTS

INTRODUCTION

This book is the attempt of two preachers to share what God has given them to understand about the study of the "magnificent obsession" of their lives. Our prayer is that the Holy Spirit will bring this into the hands of hungry preachers who want more than life to glorify Jesus Christ in their preaching. Why? We long for the whole world to know the Savior we have come to know and love so deeply; yes, that through the "foolishness of preaching" many might be saved.

It will be helpful to those who allow it. It will be helpful in the measure of the hunger the reader has for becoming a more effective preacher. Others will read it and find it uninspired, too simplistic, too conservative, too complicated, too idealistic, too cynical. For those who are teachable, while they might find it uninspired, simplistic, conservative, complicated, idealistic, or cynical, they will also find God speaking to them even through this. Hence, the miracle of grace.

It is our prayer that you, the reader, might far exceed our abilities in proclaiming the gospel so the whole world might know the marvelous grace of Jesus and that all might be saved.

CHAPTER ONE

THE SIN OF NO OPPORTUNITY

The Iron Curtain had fallen. The Soviet Union had come apart at the seams. Hungary, Latvia, Estonia, Poland and many other states were again nations governing themselves. One of the authors was invited to preach to the Estonian and Russian congregations in Tallinn, Estonia.

These were the people who had endured great hardship for the cause of Christ. These were the people who had seen loved ones taken away because of their faith, never to be seen again. These were the ones who memorized the Scripture because they could not own a Bible.

Yet when this preacher preached to the Russian congregation, he gave an invitation to receive Christ as Savior and Lord. Many came to the front to make a first-time commitment to Christ. One young Russian girl spoke English. The pastor invited the preacher to pray with her. It was his privilege to lead that young lady to Christ.

This experience is just one of numerous examples through the centuries of the central premise of this book: Proclamation of the gospel of Jesus Christ must always include an invitation for response. Never assume in any gathering of people that no one needs to respond to the gospel—perhaps for the first time. Since the gospel demands a response, someone is always waiting for the opportunity.

The gospel (good news) is an invitation, a call to action, a converting word. All of these demand a response. Indifference, neutrality and silence are not options. We either accept or reject the gospel message. We either accept or reject the Christ of the gospel. We either accept or reject the call of the gospel to us.

Jesus came preaching the gospel: "Repent, the kingdom of heaven is at hand." The parables of Jesus were confrontational and demanded a response. The Sermon on the Mount necessitated a response. Response is at the very heart of the gospel.

A recent broadcast of the worship service of a historic mainline church stirred the passions of one of these authors. The pastor of that congregation was not known to be an evangelical. The ministry of that church was mundane. The worship services were very formal and lifeless. Yet this one day the pastor brilliantly preached an evangelical message declaring the gospel of grace. This sermon demanded a response. Much to the author's surprise and disappointment the preacher ended the sermon with, "In the Name of the Father, Son, and Holy Spirit. Amen." Then he said, "Let's be sure to pray for Aunt Susie who is still in the hospital and Uncle John who is recovering at home. Are there any other prayer requests?" That was followed by the offertory prayer and the offering with doxology and benediction.

It was as if the table of God's grace had been lavishly prepared and spread before us, but no one was invited to come and partake of the goodness of God. The theological/liturgical argument was that the offering was the response. However, the offering and the prayers for the sick had absolutely nothing to do with the Scripture text or the sermon. Anyone who heard the Good News was disappointed with the lack of an invitation/opportunity to receive and embrace the good news of God's grace. If "today is the day of salvation," that service gave no opportunity for it to be received.

Warren served a small congregation in a town of just 1,100 people where half of the population was white and half was black. The village boasted a white Methodist church and a black Methodist church, a white Baptist church and a black Baptist church. Rarely did a visitor ever attend any of those churches. Most Sundays the attendees were made up of folks who had attended for many years.

Yet one dear old saint told the young preacher he needed to "open the doors of the church" every Sunday. The preacher saw no need to do so since almost everyone who attended was already a member. So he and she carried on conversations about "opening the doors of the church." What he learned was she wanted to be sure that every Sunday people were given opportunity to respond to the gospel as it was proclaimed in worship. To "open the doors of the church" was a euphemism for giving an opportunity for response.

Through her insistence the young preacher learned to find some ways for people to respond, other than simply joining the church. Most of them had already done that. But Sunday after Sunday the gospel was being preached without any thought being given to how the worshiper might want or need to respond. No thought was given to helping the worshiper live out the gospel in real, everyday ways.

These authors have a collective 17 years of formal theological education. Yet never in those years did anyone attempt to instruct either of us in how to preach for a response, how to give the invitation for a response, or even why we ought to find a way to invite and encourage a response. Yet that 80-year-old saint knew intuitively that such an opportunity needed to be given. Response is inherent in the gospel and the gospel preacher who does not invite response is not being completely faithful to the gospel.

Perhaps modern preachers need to contemplate the *Sin of No Opportunity*. How many sermons are preached, how many worship services are conducted in churches all across America without any thought being given to a response by the hearer? How often do preachers and worship leaders prepare a great banquet, set it before the people, entice them to this gospel feast with beautiful words and music, yet never say, "Come and get it?" The failure to invite response is "The Great Omission" of the modern church in America.

Preachers today tend to focus on wanting their congregation "to know" or "to understand," but rarely do they think about what they (or God) want their congregation to do or how to act. The questions need to be asked: What do I hope God will do with this message? What do I hope the hearer will do? Then, what can I (the preacher) do to invite the congregation to do in order to experience that?

The Apostle Paul certainly understood the need for response. Listen to his words in Romans 10:8-17:

> But what does it say? "The word is near you; it is in your mouth and in your heart," that is, the word of faith we are proclaiming: That if you confess with your mouth, "Jesus is Lord," and believe in your heart that God raised him from the dead, you will be saved. For it is with your heart that you believe and are justified, and it is with your mouth that you confess and are saved. As the Scripture says, "Anyone who trusts in him will never be put to shame." For there is no difference between Jew and Gentile—the same Lord is Lord of all and richly blesses all who call on him, for, "Everyone who calls on the name of the Lord will be saved." How, then, can they call on the one they have not believed in? And how can they believe in the one of whom they have not heard? And how can they hear without someone preaching to them? And how can they preach unless they are sent? As it is written, "How beautiful are the feet of those who bring good news!" But not all the Israelites accepted the good news. For Isaiah says, "Lord, who has believed our message?" Consequently, faith comes from hearing the message, and the message is heard through the word of Christ.

Several action verbs are used by Paul—*confess*, *believe*, *trust*, *call*, *accept* and *hear*. All make clear that some kind of response is necessary for the gospel to have its intended effect. Hence, it is imperative for the preacher to give listeners the opportunity to respond.

The first post-Pentecost sermon was preached by Peter. He boldly proclaimed the lordship, the messiahship, of Jesus Christ to the same people who had called for his crucifixion just 50 days before. The writer of Acts tells us, "When the people heard this, they were cut to the heart and said to Peter and the other apostles, 'Brothers, what shall we *do*?'" (Acts 2:37) [italics mine].

It was clear to the listener that such a gospel message demanded a response. Yet they did not know what to do.

We may delude ourselves into thinking that just because the listener recognizes the need to respond, that he or she will know how to make a proper response to the gospel. More likely, without direction, guidance and invitation from the preacher, most will simply make no overt, conscious, intentional response, and by failing to do so will in fact reject the message they just heard.

But Peter would not ignore their need for direction, their need for invitation. The proper response to the message he was preaching was this: "Repent and be baptized, every one of you, in the name of Jesus Christ for the forgiveness of your sins. And you will receive the gift of the Holy Spirit. The promise is for you and your children and for all who are far off—for all whom the Lord our God will call" (Acts 2: 38-39).

The opportunity to respond to the gospel was given by Peter. Also, he gave very clear instructions as to the type of response that would be appropriate. Then he told them what the result would be if they responded.

But Peter did not stop there. "With many other words he warned them; and he pleaded with them, 'Save yourselves from this corrupt generation'" (2:40).

What was the result of Peter's gospel proclamation and invitation? Here is how Acts records it: "Those who accepted his message were baptized, and about three thousand were added to their number that day" (2:41).

Fanny Crosby's "Rescue the Perishing" from earlier days of American Methodism says, "Plead with them earnestly, plead with them gently; He will forgive if they only believe. Rescue the perishing, Care for the dying; Jesus is merciful. Jesus will save."

Isn't it clear that the first disciples are our example, and they each had to respond to the invitation to follow Jesus? "As Jesus went on from there, he saw a man named Matthew sitting at the tax collector's booth. 'Follow me,' he told him, and Matthew got up and followed him" (Matthew 9:9).

Peter, James and John became disciples of Jesus after the great catch of fish. "When Simon Peter saw this, he fell at Jesus' knees and said, 'Go away from me, Lord; I am a sinful man!' For he and all his companions were astonished at the catch of fish they had taken, and so were James and John, the sons of Zebedee, Simon's partners.

"Then Jesus said to Simon, 'Don't be afraid; from now on you will catch men.' So they pulled their boats up on shore, left everything and followed him" (Luke 5:8-11).

A careful reading of the entire passage beginning in verse 5:1 reveals several responses by Peter, James and John before the response of becoming a disciple ("he said to Simon 'Put out into the deep water and let down you nets for a catch'").

So it is that many people who make a lifelong faithful commitment to Christ do so after several "smaller" responses along the way. This reveals the necessity of preaching for a response, designing the response, inviting the response that is not always so monumental as "leaving everything to follow Jesus." Most often that response of "leaving everything" is made only after several other responses have already been made along the faith-traveler's way.

One of the best studies in preaching for a response in the last 50 years is the study of Dr. Billy Graham's crusade evangelism. No doubt he is the most widely respected Christian in the world. While his crusade methods may be unique to his calling, any preacher can learn from what Dr. Graham has done so well.

There are many reasons for Dr. Billy Graham's effectiveness in reaching the unchurched: a well-run organization, the providence of God, his genuine humility, the strong emphasis on prayer, the integrity of his association and the evangelist, the use of appropriate music, and many others.

However the one reason that must not be overlooked is Dr. Graham's effective preaching for a response. In his crusades, the desired response is always the same. However, anyone who has ever been involved in a Billy Graham crusade knows that neither Dr. Graham nor anyone in his organization takes the invitation and response for granted. They plan very carefully for the response.

The last time Dr. Graham preached a crusade in Atlanta, it was held in the Georgia Dome, an arena that will seat more than 70,000 people. The Dome was filled to overflowing. Yet no chairs were set up on the floor of the Dome. Except for the stage, the floor was almost completely empty. Why? The staff of the crusade had planned and prepared for the invitation and the response. Therefore they knew they would need the entire floor to accommodate those who would respond to Dr. Graham's invitation. And just as they had planned, each night the floor of the Dome was filled with those responding to the invitation to follow Christ.

However, simply preparing the place to accommodate the invitation was not all that happened. Hundreds of volunteers had been recruited and trained to respond to the invitation and to deal with the vast number of people who would respond. A variety of languages were accommodated. A variety of ages were addressed. The team made sure when people responded that someone was there to take care of them.

But that's not all. For months thousands of volunteers had been praying for the invitation, the response. For months thousands had been telling others about the crusade to get them to attend and respond. And for months thousands had been trained to come early to the Dome, find their seats and begin praying for specific individuals to respond to the Gospel.

But perhaps the most significant preparation (other than the prayerful preparation of the heart of the preacher) is the way Dr. Graham always gives the invitation several times before he gives the actual invitation. Before he starts preaching he tells the listeners that after the sermon he will give an invitation to come to Christ and thousands of them will respond. During the sermon at least one time he will repeat this message that after the sermon he will give the invitation and they will want to respond. Then he speaks clearly and simply to the need for their response. The invitation is given and thousands walk to the front and confess their faith in Christ.

Just like every Sunday may not require "opening the doors of the church," every Sunday does not require an "invitation to receive Christ as your Lord and Savior" in the way that Dr. Graham does at his crusades. But every Sunday, every service requires the preacher to pay attention to the need for a response to the gospel message he or she is preaching, planning for and issuing the invitation to response.

All of this raises the question: "Why do most mainline preachers fail to issue an invitation or give opportunity for response?" There are several possible reasons for this. More than one may apply to any reader.

WE DO NOT REALLY BELIEVE PEOPLE ARE LOST.

Perhaps the most damnable theology to dominate modern theological education is the theology of universalism, that everyone will be saved. This heresy has made its way into the very fabric of modern theological thought and life.

"After all, how could a loving God condemn anyone to hell?" goes the Sunday school version of the question. The theological school version is more sophisticated, but no less misguided.

While the modern preacher believes the gospel can help "those less fortunate" and even can enhance the lives of those who "have it all together," we do not really believe faith is a matter of eternal life and eternal death. If we did, we would be far more concerned about the eternal lives and destinies of those residing in our mission field (beginning with one's own parish).

There resides in us the conviction that somehow everything will be OK in the end. It is the same type of myth we moderns have believed, that says the government will take care of us. Neither is true.

While most preachers do not really believe in universalism, we nevertheless act as if it were true. Perhaps what we do or fail to do says more about what we really believe than what we say we believe. Our failure to invite our listeners to make a response to the gospel is indicative of what we really believe.

WE DO NOT BELIEVE THE POWER OF THE GOSPEL.

While we believe the gospel is the answer to peace and justice issues, we do not really believe it is powerful enough to change the heart of a greedy business person, to change the heart of an abusive father or mother, to change the heart of a rebellious teenager, to change the heart of a young adult strung out on cocaine, to change the heart of an "innocent" eight-year-old child.

Certainly we wish they would change. Certainly we want to help with their "issues." Certainly we have a network of caregivers to deal with these life struggles. Counselors, mentors, big brothers, 12-step programs and institutions all offer help to the conflicted life.

But is it possible for the alcoholic to be delivered from his or her addiction "simply" through believing the gospel? Is it possible the gospel is powerful enough to deliver the greedy corporate president from the destructive life he is leading? Is it possible for the gospel to provide what is needed to get the homeless person off the street and into decent housing? Is it possible for the gospel to be strong enough to heal a broken body ravaged with cancer?

If none of that is possible, then why give an invitation to respond? If none of this can happen, why offer false hope to those who listen to our sermons? If the lame can't be healed and walk and the blind can't see again, why invite them to Jesus in the first place?

WE DO NOT KNOW HOW TO INVITE A RESPONSE.

Many of us have never witnessed effective invitations that elicit a proper response to the gospel. Our pastors do not give them. Our churches do not embrace them. Our orders of worship do not accommodate them.

Or we have witnessed ineffective or manipulative invitations. Perhaps we have seen a desperate preacher copy Billy Graham's invitation in a church with 50 people in attendance. Somehow, it just didn't work. Perhaps we have had to tolerate singing 23 verses of "Just as I Am" until someone finally responded. It could be that we have witnessed the manipulation of a congregation by the preacher resulting in inappropriate responses.

However, no other person's ineffectiveness is an excuse for my own ineffectiveness. Just because someone else gave an inappropriate or manipulative or ineffective invitation does not excuse me from the need to give proper opportunity for response. Yet since all we have witnessed has been something less than authentic, we do not know how to give an authentic invitation to response.

WE WOULD NOT KNOW WHAT TO DO IF THEY DID RESPOND.

We have each known preachers/pastors who admitted to not knowing how to lead someone to Christ. What if someone came to the preacher at the altar and said, "I want to become a Christian?" What would the pastor do? Many pastors apparently do not know what to do.

Of course, this feeling of uncertainty and inadequacy would be intensified if 10 or 15 people responded to an invitation. What would the pastor/preacher do? There is no time to speak to all of them and pray with all of them, even if he/she knows what to do. What if they really did respond, what would we do?

OUR ORDER OF WORSHIP DOES NOT ACCOMMODATE A RESPONSE.

Usually the order of worship makes no provision for response other than joining the church. Is every sermon designed to invite people to join the church? Of course not. Then why is that the only type of response we accept?

More often than not, there isn't even an opportunity to respond in that way. We preachers have been fishing in barren ponds for so long that we no longer want to be embarrassed by how little we catch each Sunday; consequently we no longer even try. If people want to become Christians, if they want to join the church, they can seek us out after the service and tell us, or better yet, call the office and let the secretary tell them how to do it.

Worship services that only and always follow the sermon with the offering usually give no avenue for response other than the offering. While response through the offering is sometimes very appropriate, usually it is not. Since no other option is given, no other invitation is offered and no other response is expected or accommodated. Does your service accommodate response?

WE ARE FEARFUL OF THE OPINION OF OTHERS.

Since most of our peers do not preach for response and most of our church members have never witnessed it being done effectively, we are afraid if we give invitations to respond to the gospel they will think less of us. We may be seen as foolish fundamentalists. We may be thought of as enthusiastic evangelicals. We may be viewed as crazy charismatics. We may be labeled as hip-hoppity holy-rollers.

No one wants to stand in opposition to the majority. When most preachers and most church members do not value an invitation to respond to the gospel, it is very uncomfortable when we give one.

Yet is preaching the gospel about popularity? Is it about pleasing church members? Is it about peer pressure? Or is it about proclaiming the everlasting truth of the gospel of Jesus Christ and inviting the hearers to respond to this gospel?

WE DO NOT TAKE PREACHING SERIOUSLY ENOUGH.

The "Saturday night special," the "internet solution" and the "preaching-book sermon" do not encourage issuing a proper invitation. They simply give the lazy or misguided preacher a way out on Sunday. But they do not burn in the heart of the one charged with the proclamation of the gospel. They do not inspire the one who is entrusted with the declaration of the "whole counsel of God."

If we are not going to prepare adequately to preach, why should we even be concerned with an invitation? We will not. Hence, inadequate preparation for preaching results in little or no invitation to respond. Laziness will defeat the preacher and destroy the opportunity for people to hear and respond to the gospel.

CHAPTER TWO

UNDERSTANDING WHY PEOPLE NEED TO RESPOND

On September 11, 2001, it seemed everything had changed. A nation watched in horror as one of the World Trade Center towers was burning from the wreckage of the airliner that crashed into it. Then before our very eyes a second plane flew into the second tower. We wept as we imagined the passengers, crews and those in the towers. We simply could not believe it when the first tower came crashing down, then the second. We heard of the crash into the Pentagon, and in Pennsylvania and we knew life would never be the same.

America was under attack, the most heinous kind of attack—terrorism, war waged against civilians, innocents, women and children. The President declared war on terrorism that day. And we somehow knew that from now on we would mark time from before 9/11 and after 9/11. It would be for this generation what Pearl Harbor was for the Builder Generation and the Kennedy assassination was to the Boomer Generation.

For two or three Sundays after 9/11 churches that normally had plenty of room at worship found their sanctuaries filling up. Churches that were normally full found they could not adequately accommodate the larger crowds. But soon the crisis was over. Attendance went back to normal in most churches. Life moved back to the routine.

But why did attendance at houses of worship increase so dramatically after 9/11? Who were these people who filled our churches and synagogues and mosques? Where did they come from? What did they want? What were they looking for?

The truth is that many of them were members who decided they had become too lazy about attendance and came back to church. Many were those who had simply drifted away. But a surprising number were people who had never turned to churches before. For the first time they came seeking comfort, hope, answers.

What did they receive? Does the fact that soon attendance was back to "normal" mean anything about what they did or did not receive? Does the church have any obligation to these "seekers" who turned to us in time of crisis? What about all those who did not turn to the church? Do we have any obligation to them? What about those who perished on 9/11, who did not know Christ? Did the church have an obligation to them? What about the people in the community, within the shadow of church steeples of our churches? Do we have an obligation to them? What about the people of Afghanistan and Pakistan and the other countries of the world? Does the church have an evangelical obligation to them?

Or is the right and proper role of the church to care for its own, meet the needs of its own, invest its resources in its own, preach to and teach its own to the effective exclusion of those who are outside the church? Is it enough for the church to continue to do "business as usual" in the face of such cataclysmic changes?

We, the church, are about two or three cataclysms behind. Most of our churches have never caught on to the changes wrought in the culture by the volcanic 1960s. So much of what we do, especially in worship, is just like we did it before the cultural revolution of the Sixties. We certainly did not make accommodation to the changes wrought by the Information Age, the MTV age, the cellphone age.

Hence, to think that the church would change in response to the change in the culture caused by 9/11 is the most optimistic of thinking. Yet that is exactly what we are: optimists of the highest order. We believe the church of Jesus Christ will change rapidly in response to 9/11 and the other cultural changes due to come our way.

Why do we believe that? Because of the emerging phenomenon of the "mission church" in America. The mission church is a church that takes responsibility for the people around it. It understands it has an obligation to the least, the last, and the lost of the world in which it exists. It invests its resources on behalf of those who are not part of the church rather than investing itself in itself. I am not using the term in its usual sense of a newly established and financially dependent church.

Those within the Wesleyan family of churches certainly should understand this distinction. One of our founders was Thomas Ware. He began his ministry in 1775. One day he was asked by a clerical opponent whether he was a missionary. "I replied," he said, "that I am a Methodist and we are all missionaries."[1]

"Clearly, American Methodism was conceived as a missionary movement calculated to win the greatest number of people in the shortest possible time."[2]

It was this comprehension of serving in mission on a mission field that prompted John Wesley to declare: "The world is my parish." For Mr. Wesley there was no parochialism, no petty denominationalism, no boundaries set by tradition and ecclesiastical authority—just mission, mission, mission.

What's different about being the church in a mission field? The answer lies in seeing what the needs of the mission field are and rediscovering what it is that the church has to offer. The mission church becomes a church for others, recognizing that its own needs are met only through meeting the needs of others. The mission church understands the words of Jesus, "Except a grain of wheat falls into the ground and dies, it abides alone, but if it dies it brings forth much fruit" (John 12:24).

NEEDS-BASED MINISTRY

The mission church does not set its own agenda. It is set by the one sheep that is lost. It is set by the naked and the hungry, the cold, the sick and the imprisoned. The mission church has its agenda set by the world in which it finds itself.

That does not mean the mission church adopts the agenda of the world. That would mean it would become self-centered. It would become a consumer. It would become materialistic. It would become hedonistic. It would become like the traditional church.

The mission church knows what it is, whose it is, and what it has to offer to the world. But the way it does its work, the way it lives its communal life, the way it exists in the world is determined by the needs of the world and not its own needs. In fact, the church that does not exist for mission is the church that becomes self-centered, consumeristic, materialistic and hedonistic. Look at the traditional church today and see if it has not succumbed to the world in spite of trying to care for its own.

The mission church is "in the world, but not of the world." It is certain of its task: to make disciples of Jesus Christ. The mission is clear. Its vision is that of a loving God who gave his only Son to redeem a lost and dying world. The mission church knows it possesses the "greatest story ever told." The mission church knows clearly who it is; it has a clearly defined mission, vision and core values.

But the mission church also knows and understands the world in which it lives. It knows the needs of the people of its community. So it designs its ministry based on their needs and not the needs of those inside the church.

The self-understanding of the mission church is the same as that of the mission station in a foreign country. Its ministries, its priorities, are for those outside the mission station, not inside. It has a clinic if the people outside the mission station need emergency medical care. It has a hospital if those outside the mission station need a hospital. It has a school if those outside the mission station need a school. Its very existence is defined by the needs of those outside the mission station.

So it is for the mission church. It invites its members, those inside the mission station, to be missionaries. It believes the only way to meet the deepest needs of its own members is in helping them invest themselves in others. It unapologetically proclaims to those inside the mission station: "We exist for others," "We are a church for others," and invites them to embrace this mission. Those who refuse can freely choose to attend another kind of church.

HOPES AND HURTS

The mission church knows that most needs can be placed in two dream baskets: one is a basket of hopes and the other is a basket of hurts. In every community there are those hurts and hopes that are universal to our human predicament. The mission church understands those dreams and attempts to touch them with real healing and hope. However, in every mission field, including the one where the reader is called to serve, there are hurts and hopes peculiar to that community.

Warren was working with a group of lay missionaries who were starting new missions in the North Georgia area. One of the newest missions is to day laborers in a city near Atlanta. The day laborers are underpaid, most have addictions, are homeless and have no means of extracting themselves from their current predicament. One lay missionary is establishing a program providing food, clothing, shelter, addiction treatment, financial counseling and psychological counseling for these men and their families. The location of the mission began in the facility of a temporary services company that employs many of these persons. It has since moved into a nearby United Methodist church. About 200 family units are being served by the mission. One year after its beginning, 28 people have been converted, six have gone home for the first time in years, hundreds are clothed and fed, many have found full-time employment and several are in alcohol and drug addiction counseling. Of course, some are in jail and some have died. However, some of those who died, died in Christ due to this ministry.

Until this mission started in 2002, no church was touching these lives. There are dozens of churches of all denominations within five miles of this mission. Yet none even recognized the needs of these people in their own community. The lay missionary is traveling 20 miles to address the needs of this constituency.

Where is the church for these men and women and their families? Why did no local mission station (church) see the need and design the ministry to meet the need? How could people be homeless and hungry and cold and imprisoned in the cells of addiction within a stone's throw of some of the most affluent churches in the world?

Warren was the lead missionary (senior minister) of a local mission station (church) that recognized the crisis of unwanted or unplanned pregnancies in mostly young women. Rather than simply giving opinions about whether abortion is right or wrong, he and other missionaries (church members) in that mission station (church) began a ministry to women in crisis. Imagine his surprise to learn that it was the only church-related crisis pregnancy center in the Metro Atlanta area. Did the other churches not have people in their communities getting pregnant out of wedlock? Did they not have young girls choosing to have their pregnancies terminated without any counsel or guidance? Did they not have youth in their schools engaged in sexual behavior at an ever younger and younger age? Were there no middle-aged women in their church who were suffering from the horror and guilt of terminating an unwanted or unwelcome pregnancy earlier in their lives? Was this need unique to this one mission site (parish)?

The Beacon of Hope Women's Center in Alpharetta, Georgia, has had a tremendous impact on many lives. Hundreds of babies have been carried to term. Some have been adopted into loving Christian families. Others have been raised by trained and supported loving mothers, often with the help of an extended family. Many women have come to faith in Christ during the long months of caring and nurture by the missionaries (volunteers) of the Women's Center. Abstinence education has been provided by invitation in many public high schools and taught by these devoted Christians.

Mission churches and missionaries know the needs of their communities and design ministries to meet those needs. They deliver real, tangible help and hope and healing to those in the community who will never likely enter the doors of the church for worship on Sunday.

Why do they do this? They are moved with compassion to address the real needs of people. They understand the passage in the gospels where Jesus was "moved with compassion when he saw the multitudes, because they were harassed and helpless, like sheep without a shepherd" (Matt. 9:36). They also see that the very next thing he did was feed them—all 5,000 of them. Why did he feed them? Because they were hungry. But it was more than meeting their physical needs. He also gave to them the Bread of Life, for he gave them himself.

SCRATCH PRINCIPLE

Jesus was willing to "scratch where folks itch" to meet more critical needs in their lives. The lame are healed and their sins are forgiven. The maniac is delivered and clothed and in his right mind and following Jesus. The adulterer asks for a drink of water and is given Living Water.

This Christ-like movement from the known and tangible to the unknown and intangible is inherent in the sacrament. He takes the bread and breaks it and gives it to his friends and says, "This is my body broken for you." He takes the cup and blesses it and gives it to them saying, "This is my blood shed for you and for many for the remission of sins." He begins with their felt needs of hunger and thirst and uses them to meet much deeper needs: forgiveness and life.

Hence, when the mission station "scratches where folks itch," it is sacramental in the truest sense of the word. Like Jesus, the mission station begins with real, felt needs, hopes and hurts and serving sacramentally it meets the deepest longings and needs of the human heart.

One of the amazing realities of the mission church meeting the real needs of real people in its mission community is the growth of the church that occurs. Dr. Kennon Callahan, the father of the Mission Church Movement, said in 1983, "The church grows directly proportional to the number of people served by that church, who will never likely join that church." That has been proved correct again and again in the great mission churches.

THE MISSION CHURCH VERSUS THE TRADITIONAL CHURCH

What are the differences between a mission station (church) and a traditional church? There are many. Here is a short list of comparisons and contrasts that illustrate how significant the differences really are.

Mission Church	**Traditional Church**
Measures Disciples Made	Measures Visits Made
Welcomes Change	Fears and Avoids Change
Focuses on Others	Focuses on Self
Becomes Personally Involved in Ministry	Sends Money to Mission
Equips and Empowers the Laity for Ministry	Sees Ministry as the Work of Professionals
Faces Conflict with Hope	Runs from Conflict
Leadership Is Missional	Leadership Is Managerial
Knows the Culture	Knows the Church

Mission Church	**Traditional Church**
Is Denominationally Faithful	Defines Everything by the Denomination
Transformational	Transactional
Permission Giving	Permission Withholding
Worship Is Participatory	Worship Is Performance
Intentionally Serves Non-members	Intentionally Serves Members
Shares the Power	Holds the Power
Trusts	Suspects
Staff Serves the Culture	Staff Serves the Church
Trusts Results	Trusts Credentials
Gives As a Response	Gives as Duty
Focuses on Grace	Focuses on Law
Culturally Appropriate Worship	Denominationally Appropriate Worship
Offers Variety of Worship Services	One-Size-Fits-All Worship
Fails Often	Seldom Fails
Succeeds Often	Seldom Succeeds
The World Is Its Parish	The Parish Is Its World
Sings from the Heart	Sings from the Head

Mission Church	Traditional Church
Cross-Cultural Ministry	Homogeneic Ministry
Evangelistic	Paternalistic
Clear Vision	Cloudy Vision
Unifying Mission	Self-Preserving Ministry
Preaches in the Language of the Culture	Preaches in the Language of the Church
Transformational Preaching	Transactional Preaching
Defines Ministry by the Mission	Defines Mission by the Ministry
Ministry	Church Work
Depends on the Holy Spirit	Depends on Tradition
Sees Problems as Opportunities	Sees Problems as Power Issues
Visitor Friendly	Member Friendly
Unchurched Friendly	Churched Friendly
Celebrates	Commemorates
Serves Food	Eats Food
Budget Based on Giving Per Attendee	Budget Based on Pledges
Offers Many Designated Giving Opportunities	Limits Most Giving to the Unified Budget
Creates	Preserves

Mission Church	Traditional Church
Starts New Ministries	Maintains Old Ministries
Optimistic	Pessimistic
Looks Forward	Looks Backward
Growing	Declining
Inclusive	Exclusive
Passionate for the Lost	Passionate for the Saved

Probably most of the readers of this book will have grown up in traditional/chapel churches and are most comfortable with the traditional approach to ministry. Therefore, the above list is disconcerting to our understanding of the church. It has been offensive to a number of people to whom it has been presented over the last 15 years.

However, what is truly offensive in the context of the gospel is that one-third to one-half of the United Methodist Churches in America do not record a single profession of faith in any given year. But more importantly, it is offensive to "the least of these" who we simply are not reaching because of our preference for things to be as they have always been. Then, certainly, it must be offensive to the God who gave his only Son. When the church is more concerned about itself, its agenda, and its comfort than it is about the lost, surely it grieves the heart of God.

Someone has said, "Insanity is doing what you have always done and expecting different results." Yet thousands of churches are more concerned with traditional approaches to church life and ministry than reaching the world for Jesus. But they do not understand why they continue to die. Traditional ministry is carried on in ever-shrinking churches in increasingly empty church buildings.

EXPERIENCE CULTURE

Because our culture is so secular and often anti-church, the church must find effective ways to speak to the unchurched and dechurched of our culture. The same old worn out sermons and liturgies will not capture the imagination or interest of a culture seeking the experience of God. This is an experience-oriented culture; hence the ESPN X-Games, the rush to bungee jumping, the faster, higher and scarier roller coasters, the increase in rock climbing and mountain climbing resulting in so many deaths each year.

The effective sermon in such a mission culture must invite the listener to experience God, not just hear about God. An intellectual exercise in theological maneuvering will frustrate and even anger those we must try to reach. Effective preaching will invite the listener to move beyond passive listening or even active listening into the experience of the transforming power of God.

In a recent seminar, Lyle Schaller reviewed Pine and Gilmore's *The Experience Economy* (Harvard Business School Press 1999). Dr. Schaller told how the authors reviewed the history of the American economy. Ours was at first a commodities-based economy (the Agrarian Age). A farmer traded eggs for flour and butter for coffee in the commodities economy. Then ours became a goods economy (Industrial Age). People paid for goods with the money they earned in factories and other places of employment. The Goods Economy was followed by the Services Economy (Services Age). This was the economy from 1950–1990. Most people were employed in the service industry. Now our economy is an Experience Economy (Experience Age). It is this age in which people are looking for significant experiences. We are no longer content to read about life in a book, or listen to soap operas on radio. Reality TV has taken over the passive entertainment. But that simply is not enough.

Examine the rapid growth of Extreme Sports, white-water rafting, racecar driving, bungee jumping, parachuting, hang-gliding, even traveling to outer space, no matter that it costs $20,000,000. A generation ago almost none of those activities were even available to the public. Today they are often demanded by the public.

The same is true of the church. People no longer simply go to church. People *do* church. They come to worship to experience something; not to observe, not to be spectators, but to have the experience of the Transcendent One. This demands that we do worship, we do church, *and* we do preaching differently than we used to do them. Why shouldn't these changes in our culture and economy also bring changes in the church? They have made changes in almost every industry and environment.

The Experienced-Based mission will accommodate the changes necessary for effectiveness. It will discard what no longer works and embrace what does. Communities used to have area swimming pools. Now we have massive water parks. Even some hotels have their own water parks. The old has been replaced with the new. Canton, Georgia, like every small town in America, had a movie theater. Now it has a Cineplex of theaters and that Cineplex will eventually be replaced by IMAX or the next generation. Churches used to give to missions. The Woman's Society for Christian Service was a place to read about mission, talk about mission, and collect money for mission. Today, churches that have a significant role in missions are those who send multiple short-term mission teams all around the world. Experience is the valued commodity in an Experience Economy.

Dr. Schaller further suggests that Pine and Gilmore are correct to predict that the emerging economy is the Transformation Economy. This is certainly the greatest opportunity the church has had in recent generations. We exist for transformation. Unfortunately, we cannot offer transformation to others until the church itself is transformed.

TRANSFORMATION

The mission church exsists in a world that is pre-Christian. It is more like the world to which the Apostle Paul ministered than like that of previous generations of mainline pastors and churches in the U.S. Secular humanism, pantheism, new ageism, syncretism, agnosticism, and self-help-ism are just a few of the symptoms of this religious/theological cultural setting. While being un-Christian and often anti-Christian, this theological milieu is indicative of the spiritual hunger and spiritual search inherent in this culture.

Orthodox Christianity is the religious expression that is least tolerated by the religious, media, educational and entertainment worlds. This has caused the church often to find herself being presented as the enemy of the community, a bad neighbor, intolerant and bigoted.

Even though much of our culture expresses open, even hostile opposition and many individuals parrot those same feelings, we should not assume that people aren't yearning for God. They certainly are. Those who make the effort to participate in a worship service have already taken a step toward change.

The mission church and the mission pastor (local missionary) must not betray them by assuming they aren't interested in transformation. They may not want to give up control. They may not want to surrender their wills; they may want to hang on to sinful habits. But at the same time, they still want to change. They struggle with this inner battle: "I do want to change, I don't want to change, I do want to change, I don't want...."

We recognize this universal desire to be something more than we are, to find meaning, purpose and fulfillment in life. Therefore the mission church and the missionary pastor must help them change. We must nudge them, prod them, challenge them, invite them. To fail to do this is to ignore completely this great need for transformation in people's lives.

It is the responsibility of the church to provide direction for those seeking The Way. It is the responsibility of the church to speak the word of truth to those who are seeking The Truth. It is the responsibility of the church to offer life to those seeking The Life.

Many who live in this pre-Christian world, this world of the mission church, are in real inner crisis. This inner crisis shows itself most clearly in the conflicted individual. These are the people who want to do better, to do what is right, to live by higher and truer standards, but just cannot seem to do so. This can be clearly seen in parents who desire to be the best they can be, yet they still smoke around their kids, still divorce, still teach poor financial management. They want to do the right thing, but somehow cannot.

These conflicted individuals understand Paul's lament in Romans, "O wretched man that I am! Who will deliver me from this body of sin and death!" (Romans 7:24). Yet they have not come to know the truth of Paul's great affirmation in Romans 7:24, "Thanks be to God through Jesus Christ our Lord," and Romans 8:1, "There is therefore now no condemnation to those who are in Christ Jesus."

The mission church assumes people have an innate hunger for God. It assumes that given the right opportunity, most people will respond to the grace of God in Christ. While depending on the work of prevenient grace, it believes it has the responsibility to invite, engage, encourage, and urge a response of faith on the part of the listener. It does not assume that just because they are in church, they have experienced the transforming power of the gospel. The mission church sees every person as an opportunity for grace, and takes responsibility for declaring that grace and inviting the recipient of grace to be transformed by its power.

Preaching for a response assumes responsibility for inviting people to respond in ways that are authentic and appropriate to the gospel. It does not assume that people will make their own response. It responsibly leads them to a response—and to multiple responses, building in intensity of faith and commitment.

This preaching acknowledges and encourages the desire of the listener to experience transformation. Only the most conservative traditionalist is unable to see this innate desire being evidenced in today's world.

The Prayer of Jabez sold millions of copies and spent months on the *New York Times* Best Seller list. This little book is all about transformation and the buying public cleaned it off the shelves.

Rick Warren's *Purpose Driven Life* captured the imagination of the church and the secular world and sold multiple millions.

Folks desire to be changed, to be transformed. Will the church, will the preacher, will the worship service, will the sermon offer any less?

The work of the church has always been and still is the work of transformation. We measure the effectiveness of the church by the number of lives changed, not dollars raised, buildings built, staff employed, or good causes supported. We are invited to embrace the call of transformation—the changing of lives and destinies.

The United Methodist Church states this belief in its *Book of Discipline*: "The United Methodist Church believes today, as Methodism has from the first, that the only infallible proof of a true church of Christ is its ability to seek and to save the lost, to disseminate the Pentecostal Spirit and life, to spread Scriptural holiness, and to transform all peoples and nations through the gospel of Christ."

PREACHING IN THE MISSION CHURCH

People are yearning for God, yearning for change, yearning for transformation. The mission field requires a different way of thinking, of being and doing, of preaching and worship.

The effective sermon in such a mission culture will invite the listener to experience God, not just hear about God. An intellectual exercise in theological maneuvering will frustrate and even anger those we must try to reach. Effective preaching will invite the listener to move beyond passive listening or even active listening into the experience of the transforming power of God.

Once the church in America understands it exists for mission (and its mission is changed lives) it must understand worship and preaching are done differently in the mission church than in the traditional church. John Wesley, founder of Methodism, understood ministry in a mission church. He also understood such ministry had to change profoundly the way the church conducted worship and the way sermons were prepared and delivered. He understood ministry in the mission field.

On Sunday, June 13, 1779, Wesley attended worship in a Presbyterian church in Aberdeen, Scotland. Here is his comment,

> This very day I heard many excellent truths delivered in the kirk; but, as there was no application, it was likely to do as much good as the singing of a lark. I wonder the pious ministers of Scotland are not sensible of this. They cannot but see that no sinners are convinced of sin, none converted to God, by this way of preaching. How strange is it, then, that neither reason nor experience teaches them to take a better way![3]

The church in America finds itself called to minister in a mission field not unlike the eighteenth century or the first century. Read the accounts of the ministry of Paul as he traveled around Asia and Europe. You will discover a missionary conducting ministry in ways which were effective in reaching the people of the culture to which he was called.

We are called to minister in a world that has a smorgasbord or cafeteria spirituality. This is a "build your own theology" world. New Age spiritualism and syncretism are as viable as orthodox Christianity. The only test for authenticity is whether or not an adherent is sincere.

This has come about in a world that innately owns the emptiness of modern life. Our pace quickens, but meaning dissipates.

We have discovered the futility of materialism. It is just vanity. Those who have seen the average size of new houses grow by 20% in the last five years know that somehow, more is not better. While we still live in an economic world that is consumer driven, we also know the emptiness of having more and more.

The failure of the government to eradicate social problems has caused the public to look elsewhere for answers. If Uncle Sam cannot even fix the Social Security system, why would we expect government to fix education or homelessness or poverty?

The persistence of poverty and crime, terrorism and the threat of war have caused us to lose confidence in anyone's ability to fix what is wrong in our world. No one seems to have the answers—at least no one we previously trusted to have them. Therefore, we are forced to look to other sources of help and understanding and solace.

This is all exacerbated by the deterioration of the family. Many people find themselves the product of not just one failed family, but two or three or even five. This destruction of the basic unit of social life has left many without a social compass, a moral compass, a spiritual compass.

All of this has combined to produce a collective longing for *truth*, for *meaning*, *purpose* for *something greater*, for *hope*. Our world has rejected any notion of absolute truth. In the vacuum that has been created, people look for any truth, any meaning, any purpose, any hope.

The Mission Church deals in *hope* and *meaning*, as Abelard said, "That than which no greater can be conceived."

Even in this pre-Christian, anti-Christian world people still look to the church for answers. Some come to the church as "the option." Others come to "an option." Nevertheless, they come looking for life, looking for transformation, looking for the experience of the divine.

"Is there a word from the Lord?" That is what they want to know. And when they ask that, they look to *you*! You are the one to get up on Sundays and propose to have a word from God. Do *you*?

Is it a word of *hope*, *meaning*, *something greater* than themselves and ourselves? Or is it the same old canned drivel we have been serving for the last 50 years in the American church?

THE HARD WORK OF PREACHING IN THE MISSION FIELD

It takes work, daily hard work, to know the Lord in the intimacy of personal holiness. It certainly is not easy for the preacher/missionary serving on the modern American mission field. There are so many demands on one's time made by the traditional church—demands that can destroy the depth of the relationship one needs to have with Christ if one is to be an effective missionary/preacher. Knowing Christ is serious business.

"Herein is the compulsion of evangelism: a sense of human need may move us to care, and duty may call us to get involved, but supremely it is the adoring love of Jesus that makes us evangels of the gospel."[4]

It is this adoring love of Jesus that must be nurtured and cared for if we are going to be effective preachers. And it takes work to grow that relationship.

But it takes even more work to proclaim his Word effectively. The hard work of sermon research, prayer, meditation, planning, composition, practice, and constant improvement can never be easy. One of the reasons there are so few excellent preachers is too few are willing to do the hard, hard work of becoming excellent.

While it takes a great deal of work to preach effectively in the church, it takes still more work to communicate with mission field people. These folks don't know the Bible, or church history, or even the meaning of the language we speak in the church. The only meaning they know of redemption is the redemption of winning lottery tickets. The only meaning of "getting saved" they understand is as one young man said, "My uncle saved me from drowning last summer."

Folks on the mission field also don't have much spiritual savvy. They are often so gullible, often so hungry, they will eat anything. They do not know the difference between the chaff and the wheat. Hence, they will see *Conversations with God* as significant as The Lord's Prayer.[5]

Therefore, it is imperative that the preacher/missionary speak a clear and definitive word to a confused and hungry people. For once they "taste and see that the Lord is good," they will not be satisfied with the rice cakes of the culture.

How do we bridge the gap between God and his ways and a people who are often at best a blank slate; at worst cynical critics of all things non-material? That is the hard work of preaching on the mission field and the reason for writing a book such as this. People need the Lord. People are seeking truth, meaning, and life. Will the preacher deliver?

[1] Robert Coleman, "Nothing to do but Save Souls," *Good News* (November-December, 1998): 13.

[2] Ibid.

[3] The Works of John Wesley, ed. Richard P. Heitzenrater, 7 vols. (Nashville: Abington Press, 1988-2003) 7:135-136.

[4] Coleman, p. 12

[5] Neale Donald Walsch, Conversations with God (Putnam, 1996).

CHAPTER THREE

FOCUS—WHAT THEN SHALL I SAY?

If we are going to find effective ways to communicate the gospel in the mission field to which God has assigned us we will have to do the hard work of clearly defining the focus of each sermon. The quality sermon will be determined by the clarity of the focus.

Discovering the focus of the sermon is essential to effective, transformational preaching.[1] This focus gets the preacher and the congregation to the point of the message. The focus is not an outline. It is not the concepts contained within the text. The focus is that primary point the sermon will address.

There is no question that a specific text may elicit a variety of lessons, learnings, ideas and concepts. In previous generations it was not uncommon for preachers to expound on a variety of points within the text. The teaching points were often incongruous, but because they were found in the text, the preacher felt a duty to expound on all of them anyway. Then in the most recent generation of preachers it was not uncommon to use the text to give a multipoint "how-to" sermon on successful living.

However, effective preaching today will discover the central focus the preacher will address in the sermon. It is this focus that will shape the form and function of the sermon.

Think of the sermon as a funnel, taking all the thoughts, all the material, all the text and funneling them down to one point. That is the focus. Know that focus before preparation of the sermon. State that focus before writing anything else. State the focus in one sentence.

HOW DO YOU FIND THE FOCUS?

Discovering the focus calls for thorough exegesis. It invites scriptural exegesis. Know the text. It is through careful study of the Scripture that one comes to know the message of the text and discovers the message God is calling forth for the sermon.

Textual exegesis can be complete only when conducted in the literary, geographical, social, cultural context. This will protect both the preacher and the listener from the scriptural isolationism of many modern preachers.

However, exegesis of the text alone is not enough. Effective preaching invites cultural exegesis as well. Know the culture. The preacher must know the cultural context in which the sermon is to be preached. This cultural context will determine much of the content of the sermon since the content must be easily understandable in that culture.

Scriptural exegesis and cultural exegesis still are not enough. Effective preaching also calls for congregational exegesis. Know the listeners. Just as one must spend time with the text, so must one also spend time with the people. However, spending time with the people is no excuse for failing to spend adequate time with the text.

Dr. Fred Craddock, that great preacher and teacher of preachers (and teacher of the authors of this text) says very clearly that "time with the Bible in preparation for preaching is time with people." That is because the Bible is a real book about real people dealing with the real life issues universal to any time and place.

Finally, the effective sermon will also thoroughly exegete the context of the preacher's life. No sermon is prepared or delivered in a vacuum. Effective preaching grows out of real life—and that includes the real life of the preacher. His or her life experiences will influence the focus of the sermon.

Therefore, through excellent textual, contextual, cultural, congregational and personal exegesis the preacher determines the focus. The focus of the sermon is what the text has to say in the cultural and the congregational contexts to which the preacher is proclaiming the gospel of Jesus Christ.

So within the text and the context the focus of some familiar Scripture texts might be:

The Prodigal Son—The love and acceptance of God
The Rich Young Ruler—The cost of discipleship
The Woman with the Box of Ointment—The extravagance of grace
The Feeding of the 5,000—Jesus' compassion for the multitude
The Woman at the Well—Living Water
Nicodemus—The new birth
The Raising of Lazarus—Life in Christ
Joseph—The Providence of God
Creation Stories—The creative God
David and Absalom—The nature of friendship
Isaiah 6—"Whom shall I send?"—God's call
Three Hebrew Children—God's presence in trouble

The above does not assume the stated focus is the only focus one could find in the text. Consider the story of Zacchaeus in Luke 19:1-10. Here are four examples of a focus that might be derived from this story:

1. Heart revealed by what we do with our assets
2. Appearances can be deceiving
3. Seeking is a two-way street—Jesus seeking us, our seeking Him

4. Jesus brings real change to our lives

However, the effective sermon will choose the focus that will be addressed within the cultural and congregational context as well as the heart of the preacher. This is the genius of effective preaching.

WHAT PROCESS DO WE FOLLOW?

If we are therefore to be effective preachers we must develop a workable process, an effective method in order for our preaching and our lives to be formed by the Word of God. This demands a life of study, prayer and reflection. It is necessary, even vital, to dig a well if we are to have something to draw from.

Below is a process developed by Dr. David Bartlett and modified by Dr. Allen Hunt, both of Yale Divinity School, giving guidance for preachers who want to adequately exegete scripture.[2] It is given here as a model for anyone who desires to be both more effective in preaching and more faithful to the message of the Bible.

BASIC EXEGESIS FOR PREACHERS

Considering What I Will Say
First: What does the biblical text say?
Focus: What will I say?
Function: What will the message do?
Form: How will I say it?
Plan in advance. Select the text.

Read the text in several translations (e.g., NIV, NRSV, KJV). If you know another language, read the text in that language and compare it to the English.

Set the limits of the passage. The lectionary is not always inspired on this issue.

As you compare translations, note key words or difficult issues, issues of grammar, syntax, and structure that you will want to check.

Write down thoughts and questions that come to mind as you read the passage. What intrigues you or attracts your attention?

Examine the form of the passage. Is it a classic category like a prophecy or a parable? Does this help you understand its setting and function?

Find initial clues to the historical background of the text. A good study Bible will have notes to help with this issue.

Back off and read the passage through the larger context of the whole chapter and book if possible. Gain a sense of the whole literary context.

Note some questions that the passage raises. A Bible dictionary may help answer basic questions (e.g., What is the Praetorian Guard?).

Note how the passage relates to its larger context. A concordance will be helpful here to link the text to the rest of the book.

Are there other places in this book or the Bible where similar themes come to mind? Begin to consider all the possibilities. Gospel and Pauline parallels may help here. Seek an understanding of the theological issues and context.

Think about your congregation, its needs, its questions. Let these be a part of your considerations, but don't jump to a theme for the sermon too quickly.

Read commentaries on the passage. Try to answer any questions you may have about the passage. Be prepared to argue with the commentary and to change your mind.

Formulate in a sentence (perhaps two) what you think is central to this passage. This is not necessarily the meaning of the passage, but a sense of theme and purpose.

Find your own point of contact with the passage (e.g., seek a balance between identifying with Jesus, the disciples, a leper and the Pharisees).

Begin to think toward a focus for your message. This is the beginning of a conversation between you, the text, God, and your people. Ask: What do I hope God will do through this message?

What does God want to say through me and this text to the church and through the church to the world?

TRANSACTIONAL OR TRANSFORMATIONAL PREACHING?

After a thorough exegesis of the text, the context, the culture, the congregation and the preacher's own life, effective preaching works to create a transformation through the experience of preaching. This is the primary difference between transactional and transformational preaching.

The goal of transactional preaching is to transact a transfer of knowledge or information or even motivation. The preacher is satisfied if the listener "gets it." It is very Western and intellectual in its approach. The assumption of transactional preaching is that "getting" the message is the highest goal of effective preaching.

Transformational preaching, on the other hand, is not satisfied simply with the listener understanding or getting the message. Effective communication is not enough. The effective transformational sermon results in transformed lives. Anything less than transformation is a less than adequate effort in effective preaching.

Hence, transformational preaching requires more than complete sentences, adequate exegesis, poetic prose or entertaining methodology. It requires the creation of an experience. For it is the experience that results in change or transformation. How does the preacher create the experience desired in preaching?

CREATING AN EXPERIENCE IN PREACHING

We mean by "creating an experience in preaching" to create a world and an experience for the listener that will allow the message to sink into a level that will serve the function that you're hoping to achieve. And that function is to appeal not simply to the intellect with concepts and propositions, but to indeed create a holistic experience that would include the emotions and even some of the senses, if possible, to create a world for the listener to enter into.

One way that we did that at Mount Pisgah was in the series on

"How God Meets Your Deepest Needs." One of the sermons was "The Lord Is Your Shepherd," preaching on Psalm 23. The typical Psalm 23 sermon talks about what a shepherd did—cared for the flock, tended the flock, protected the flock, fed the flock—one usually mentions what sheep are like, describing sheep as not very bright and needing constant care and attention.

Understanding what the typical Psalm 23 sermon looked like, we then worked on a message that created an experience for people to understand not only what it means to have a shepherd, but also what it feels like and why we all need a shepherd.

In summary, we focused on the fact that people at some point in their lives will discover that they have a deep, deep spiritual need to have a divine shepherd and the strength that knowledge and awareness provides. So we structured the sermon roughly around the refrain, "You Never Know When You're Going to Need a Shepherd." This was to help people realize that life can literally turn in a second. We almost never have advance warning of when that second is going to come, and to use an old preacher phrase, "dig the well before you're thirsty." It's important to know the shepherd before you find the valley.

MOVING FROM THE FOCUS TO THE EXPERIENCE

We did that by essentially describing (obviously changing the names and with permission) three experiences that the preacher had as a pastor with people whose lives had literally changed either in a day or in a moment. The living through these three stories by the preacher and the congregation created the experience of preaching.

The first experience was that of a man in the congregation who had been working with the same firm for 18 or 20 years and had done well, as had the firm. One Monday morning he went to his office and discovered that the president of the company had stopped by his office to let him know that he would no longer have a position there, nor would several hundred other people. The door that had been open for so many years and had been one of the centerpieces of his life was now closed. He spoke of that to his pastor along with several dozen other people in the congregation. Many told him that they would pray for him and that God would open new doors and possibilities. A week or two later, we inquired how it was going. He responded, "God will provide." You never know when you're going to need a shepherd.

The preacher next described a family in a former congregation where the wife went to work one day and attended a birthday party at lunch. Five of them got into the same car. Two in the front, three in the back, with her in the middle of the back seat. It was pouring down rain as they drove to the restaurant when a car pulled out in front of them, causing them to collide with that car full force. No one was injured except her. She was thrown through the windshield and became, and still is, a quadriplegic. The preacher was able to share that family's experiences of how God walked alongside them and lifted them up and cared for them and how their faith provided hope in the dark valley. You never know when you're going to need a shepherd.

We capped the sermon with the story of Rob Holbrook's death. Rob was in his mid-twenties and at the very top of his life. He had a new girlfriend. He and his father were engaged in a successful business together. He was in great physical shape. Rob's father, Bob Holbrook, is a good friend to both of us. He and Barbara had been key people in the life and ministry of Mount Pisgah UMC, where Barbara had served as minister of music for 25 years. Bob allowed the preacher to share some of his experiences surrounding Rob's death.

All of these stories were told to try and create an experience for people, revealing the unpredictability of life, what the uncertainty of life will look like, and the simple fact of how that uncertainty feels. We emphasized what a lifesaving and life-changing experience it is to have the Lord as your Shepherd. The goal was to create an environment for the listeners so that they were drawn into a world different from the world in which they live, to help them understand something outside their own experience that they could translate and assimilate into their own lives. We wanted to create a preaching experience for them in which they were drawn in and shaped by the grace of God in a way deeper than simply pointing out the key attributes of the Shepherd.

Below is a detailed outline of the sermon written to create the experience of having such a Shepherd. Dr. Hunt does not write a full manuscript and preaches without notes. This represents the flow of the sermon he committed to memory before preaching. It is given here to provide concrete expression of how to create the kind of sermon that results in transformation.

AN EXAMPLE OF TRANSFORMATIONAL PREACHING

God Is Your Shepherd
Psalm 23

Focus: How God Meets Your Deepest Needs

Sat by the pool with my mother this week
Discussing lots of things – cancer, death, investments, life, preaching

Psalm 23 – I shared with her that I struggle with preaching the Psalms – not sure why
Love to pray from the Psalms but preaching from them is always a struggle
Asked her what she thought – Psalm 23
She said, "Reassuring"
Whatchamean?
"When I'm in the waiting room, or the doctor's office, or the hospital – I recite the words. I find them reassuring."

She's right you know – The Lord is your Shepherd – it is true - thank goodness
I have learned a little bit in the ministry – boils down to a few things

Life is fragile
Can turn in a moment – in a heartbeat, a phone call, in an instant
Dig the well before you are thirsty
Or as this psalm would say, "Know the Shepherd before you find the valley"

Because you never know when you're gonna need a shepherd

But as I tried to figure out how to share that with you—about one of your deepest needs, I ran into trouble

This need is so deep that I cannot communicate it

How do you talk about something so deep, so profound, so divine—when we are mere mortals?

I found that out with Oscar
Oscar and Mary had been married for years
Endured a lot of struggles
Pulling themselves up by their bootstraps—he working at Southwire, she at the bank
Saving, pinching—neither having been to college, neither having anything or anyone else to fall back on—just themselves
Oscar built their house—literally
Brick by brick, roof, drywall, carpet—he did it all – by himself
After work, at night, in the dark, on weekends—he built it
They had two children
One went to Georgia Tech—she is a near genius engineer

The other became a builder—some skills you just pick up
Grandchildren began to arrive—at last count there were five
One day several years back, Mary went to work—regular day
One of her co-worker's birthdays—so tellers were going to lunch to celebrate together
Rainy day—and they all five piled in the same car
two in the front—three in the back—Mary in the middle
Heading for the restaurant when a car pulled out in front of them
Driver hit the brakes—too late as slammed into the car—four of the women were fine
Mary thrown through the windshield
Oscar arrived at the hospital—shortly thereafter the pastor did too
Oscar greeted the pastor—"Preacher, we've got a little problem"
The "little problem" was the fact that Mary was now a quadriplegic
Paralyzed from the neck down—completely lucid but completely helpless
Life had changed in an instant
Not sure how he did it—but Oscar converted their home to a rehab facility
Built every kind of machine imaginable just as he had built the house
If his mind could conceive it, he built it—in the hopes of helping her regain any kind of movement or strength
So they worked—year in and year out for four years—a little progress here and there—not much but every gain was a victory
They worked and they prayed—for courage, for strength, for progress, for comfort, for assurance
They prayed, they worshiped, they built a ramp at the church, they leaned on the strength and power of God as never before
Once when I was preaching—I looked out
Saw Oscar, head down in his hands, near the back, motionless

for most of the sermon
Afterward, poked a little at him about sleeping
"Some folks call it sleeping; I call it praying."
All he said—how he coped, I can only guesstimate but it was clear—the Lord was His shepherd

Thank goodness we have a Shepherd—because you never know when you will need Him

Yea, though I walk through the valley of the shadow of death, I will fear no evil, for Thou art with me; Thy rod and staff, they comfort me.
Can get awfully dark in that valley
Thank goodness, we have a Shepherd
For you never know when you are gonna need one

Fred went to work—same as he had for 23 years
Same firm—a rarity in this modern culture of ours
Had been productive—had risen through the ranks
Now respected as a leader at the firm
When the president stopped by for a chat
Started using that language that speaks without really speaking
"There are going to be some changes."
"We are having a difficult time."
"Sales are not as we had anticipated."
"Having to do some restructuring."
By the end, Fred knew—what had been a successful and prosperous job was no more
He had three months severance to soften the blow
But everything he knew, had worked for, had hoped—gone
Life had changed in an instant
Saw him a few weeks later—shared my concerns, my hopes, my heart
He told me not to worry—"God will provide"

Usually sounds like a cliché—but this time it didn't
Words uttered in faith—because Fred knew the Shepherd

Yea, though I walk through the valley of the shadow of death, I will fear no evil, for Thou art with me. Thy rod and thy staff they comfort me.
Seem like mere words—until the Shepherd appears
Walking alongside

Funny thing about shepherds—most of time, sheep don't even notice there is one
Shepherd shows up at key times—rest of time one watches from a distance
Prepares fields for grazing—removes poisonous weeds, snakes, scorpions
Fends off enemies, attacks—wolves, bears
Comes to the aid of the sick and the wounded sheep
And guides through the dark valley—Companion and Guide in the darkest spots
Thank goodness we have a Shepherd

Robbie was excited about showing off his new girlfriend to his family
Had been dating for several months—she had begun to tame the wild stallion
His heart had begun to stir for God—in a new way, in a fresh way
So they met for a week at the beach—parents and son
How do you describe what happened next?
I thank Bob Holbrook for letting me try—that is a special privilege
They went scuba diving—as had done dozens of times
Favorite pastime for father and son
Women stayed on the beach

Dived and dived—until final dive of the day
Dad stayed on the boat—son went in for one last dive
When the son didn't come up with the group—father's spirit knew
When the guide came up with Robbie—father knew
Something had happened, something had gone horribly wrong, may never know the details and in a way details are not the issue, are they?
Robbie Holbrook was dead—in his mid-20s
How do you cope with a morass that deep?
How do you survive a valley that dark?
How do you even get up the next day?

Bob and I speak often—special ministry project of mine—I like pagans (humor)
Recently, he described it this way
"It was immediate. I had an enormous revelation of Christ, that He was with us, right there on the boat."
How did you know? What was it like?
"I cannot describe it, but just that I didn't die on the spot. Could feel His presence.
There is a Presence that carries us through. How can you experience a loss that great, that deep, of someone you love and cherish beyond words, without the support of your God? No way to survive that without Christ. There is no way."

Been a year now—since finality of life slammed in the face of Bob and Barbara and Kay and family
Been a year since the stuff that happens "to everybody else" happened firsthand
Today Bob will tell you that he is not alone. Presence that is with him. Presence that really cannot be captured in words or even in a story like this.
But if you ask, he'll tell you, "The Shepherd is with me. Thank

goodness the Shepherd is with me."
He'll tell you that that is a life-saving message

One of your deepest needs—may not even know it—perhaps your deepest need of all
A shepherd who will guide you through the valley
Do you know the Shepherd?

Recite Psalm 23 together (projected on screen)

Pray:
Lord, I need you.
By my side,
In my life,
I need you.
Today I invite you to be my Shepherd.
Come, Lord Jesus, into my life.
Amen

The sermon is included to illustrate the issue of carefully finding the focus of the sermon and then building the entire preaching experience around that focus. It is an excellent example of the premise of this book, *Preaching for a Response.*

The authors have very different styles, but God has blessed their preaching with the fruit of transformed lives. This simply illustrates the truth that there is no one "correct" way of preaching. God blesses faithful preaching, especially when the intent is transformation.

1. Allen Hunt shared "Focus, Form and Function" in the North Georgia License for Ministry School in 2001.

2. Ibid.

CHAPTER FOUR

FUNCTION—WHAT IS GOD INVITING US TO DO?

Once we know God's message (the focus) then we begin praying, "What do I hope God will do in the hearts and lives of listeners with this message?" We also pray, "What does God want them to do in response to this message?" What is the *function* of the sermon?

A helpful exercise is to enter the room where the sermon will be preached, either by actually entering the room or entering it in prayer. As you pray, visualize the service with the people seated in the seats. Live with the congregation and with the sermon as it is proclaimed to this prayer target. Ask, "What does John need to do in response to this sermon?" "What does Juanita need to do in response to this sermon?" Actually visualize these people as you pray, seeking God's guidance in determining the function of the sermon.

Just as we must be able to state in one sentence the focus of the sermon, so we must also be able to state the function. This is the statement of the response we will ask the hearer to make. Do not confuse the function with the form the invitation to response will take. That invitation will be specific and concrete and will effectively reflect the function of the sermon.

In the previous chapter was an example of a sermon with focus. The function of that sermon was to lead the listener to invite the

Shepherd into his or her life. It was really a call to put one's trust in the Shepherd before one goes through the valley and really needs the Shepherd.

It was preached in a congregation and community where people seemingly have it "all together." This upwardly mobile, affluent congregation often consists primarily of those who have had a relatively easy time in life. The preacher understood that eventually changes and challenges come to every life. The listeners experienced through the sermon the uncertainty and the hurt of life—lives similar to their own. Therefore the need for a Shepherd may not have occurred to the listener before hearing this sermon. Hence, the preacher made a strong appeal for folks to invite the Shepherd into their lives.

WHAT AM I BEING ASKED TO DO?

What is the text saying and what am I being asked to do in response to the text? This is transformational preaching. This is devotional preaching. This is life-application preaching. What is the response to which the gospel is inviting me?

Does this sermon ask the listener to:
Reflect?
Pray?
Write?
Give?
Act?
Forgive someone?
Write someone?
Call someone?
Feed someone?
Build a house?

AN ACT OF OBEDIENCE

How do we help people make a response to the Word of God?

The deed of obedience will take care of itself, once the battle of the will is won. Is not the sermon the proper place to invite people to hear a gospel that demands such a radical response? And is it not appropriate for the preacher to plan the entire service, including the sermon, to move the listener to response? Hearing is not enough. There must be a doing. There must be a surrender of the will to the will of God.

Even Jesus had to deal with this issue. In the garden of Gethsemane he was faced with a choice, a response to God's call upon his life. He did not desire to drink the cup, but he was willing. In a sense, our salvation was won in the Garden as much as on the cross. Once Jesus decided to drink the bitter cup of his own death, his death was done. When he was hauled before Pilate and charged with insurgency, he didn't have to defend himself against the charges. He had made his decision. He had responded to God's call on his life. When they mocked and beat him, he did not have to respond. He had already responded in the garden. When they nailed him to the tree, he did not need to protest. The battle was won in Gethsemane. It just had to be finished. And the work was finished on the cross of Calvary.

If Jesus had these times of response and commitment, shouldn't we assume that people today need those same opportunities? We live in a world of confusing theologies, misguided syncretism, secular do-goodism, pantheism, New Age-ism, pop psycho-babble, and little authentic direction in spiritual things. Perhaps the only time a person in our culture will ever be confronted with the claims of Christ is in worship in our church. How can we fail to design the service to lead our people to a point of decision in response to the gospel we proclaim?

ADEQUATE PLANNING

Therefore, it is imperative for effective preachers to determine the function of each sermon and adequately plan for the desired appropriate response. This planning takes into account the setting of the worship experience, the context of the sermon within the series of messages currently being preached, the context of the sermon within the entire worship experience and the tools needed to make the desired response.

THE SETTING OF THE WORSHIP SERVICE

The planning of the desired response must take into account the setting of the worship service in which the invitation to response will be made. Certain settings invite certain kinds of response and other settings discourage response. For example, response is not encouraged in a setting with a very small chancel area at the front of the sanctuary, if the desired response is for most of the congregation to come to the front of the sanctuary. Churches with very long pews discourage a response that requires movement out of the pews unless everyone is going to respond, such as with Communion served at the altar.

On one occasion one of the authors was conducting the pledge Sunday of a very important and challenging capital campaign. The church had grown so large that the congregation could not meet together for a single service. We were conducting seven weekly worship services. No facility within 20 miles could accommodate the congregation on a Sunday morning. Therefore, the church board decided to conduct the service in a large circus tent. While much could be written both about the agony and the ecstasy of this decision, for the purpose of this book the primary concern is the response.

The pastor decided that the focus and function of the sermon required the listener to fill out a pledge card and then bring it to the front and place it in one of several large baskets. Unfortunately, he had failed adequately to appraise the setting. When the 3,000 rented chairs were set up on Saturday the rows were placed very close together and each row was at least 20 chairs long. When it came time for an individual or a family to bring their card forward. it was simply impossible. There was no way they could step over or around the other people in the row. The spontaneous response desired when each person or family finished filling out the card became a colossal non-response, simply because of inadequately appraising the setting for the service. A simple solution would have been to have everyone hold the card until all had finished filling it out and then inviting them to bring it forward by rows, with everyone moving, or by simply passing baskets among the seated congregation to receive the cards of response.

Therefore, we learned the great importance of an accurate appraisal of the setting of the service and of making the desired response match that setting. General consensus was that this particular error cost the church several thousands of dollars in pledges. More importantly, it robbed several individuals of the opportunity to respond to the message of the gospel proclaimed that day.

CONTEXT WITHIN THE SERIES

Most sermons are preached within a series, whether it is the series for the liturgical year or a planned series of sermons built around a common theme, or the accidental series that results from inadequate planning or a failure to plan. Congregations share a common life, especially through worship. Therefore, stages of response can be built into a sermon series.

The level of intensity of the desired response can be built from one sermon to the next, climaxing in a very intense and significant response to the gospel. For instance, the first sermon in a series on salvation through faith in Christ might begin with an exploration of prevenient grace. The desired response may be for the congregant to make a list of the ways God has reached out in love to him or her throughout his or her life.

The second sermon might focus on our gratitude to God for his prevenient grace given to us. The congregation might be invited to write a note of gratitude to someone who has had a significant positive influence on their life.

The third sermon might deal with the human predicament of

sin. A possible response is to lead the listeners to own the reality of one's own sinfulness. This could be done through a guided prayer of confession after the sermon.

The next sermon in the series could focus on God's redemptive act in Jesus Christ. The congregation might be invited to join in singing some meaningful praise songs that glorify Jesus for His sacrifice of love on our behalf.

The final sermon in the series may lift up the need for each one to have a personal relationship with Jesus. The response might be to come to the altar and stand for a prayer by the pastor in which the respondent makes a public profession of faith in Christ. The crescendo of response aids the listener in moving toward an action that has transforming power in his or her life.

CONTEXT WITHIN THE WORSHIP SERVICE

Unfortunately, many Protestant worship services are planned by parties oblivious to the need for an invitation to respond to the gospel message. Whether it is the director of worship, the senior minister, the minister of music, the lead associate or all of the above, attention must be given by those who plan worship to include a proper opportunity for response to the message proclaimed in that service. This requires planning, a team approach to worship and a common understanding of the focus and the function of the message of the day. The focus of the message must be conveyed through the music, prayers, offering, announcements, affirmations, liturgical dance, drama, sermon and other acts of worship.

Therefore, if the function of the sermon is to lead the congregation to active participation in and a transforming experience of Holy Communion, it is assumed that the Lord's Supper must be included in the order of worship. Yet, unfortunately the disjointed or uniform orders of worship followed by most of our services will not allow for such a change to occur. In many United Methodist churches the tradition is to celebrate the Lord's Supper on the first Sunday of each month. What if the function dictated by the service on the third Sunday called for Holy Communion as the vehicle of response? Would the service include it? If it did, then how?

TOOLS NECESSARY FOR RESPONSE

Perhaps the function called forth from this sermon is to identify with the hurting. Therefore, we might make a list of people we know who have recently lost their jobs. Has the worship planning team asked the following questions?

> How can we provide the correct type of form on which to write?
> How will we get the forms into the hands of the listeners?
> How will we provide pencils or pens?
> How much time will we allow for the response?
> What will we do during that time?

All of this has to do with the very practical aspects of planning for effective worship. However, it is missing from most worship services. Inadequate planning, provision, and preparation result in little or no response even when it is invited. Only the most aggressive personalities respond to the call when we fail to provide easy access to response.

"A tool for every job and a job for every tool." That practical axiom has particular merit in inviting an appropriate response to the preaching of the gospel. A hammer is an inappropriate tool for writing a letter. A chisel does not make a good toothbrush. The appropriate use of the tools of response make the response far more effective and life changing. Keep your tools sharp and ready for the occasion when God will touch the lives of the people God is calling to Christ. Provide the congregation with the tools of response they need to facilitate their making an appropriate response to the life-changing message of the gospel of Christ.

USE CAUTION!

Certainly there is a danger in preaching for response. Be cautious because this can be done without integrity and the response can be incongruent with the gospel.

Preachers and worship leaders can manipulate a congregation into making the kinds of response that are self-serving and lack the power of the gospel to transform the hearers' lives. Inappropriate responses certainly devalue the gospel message and should never be used by the preacher who values the integrity of the gospel.

However, the abuse of the invitation, the manipulation of a congregation and the exploitation of the gospel by unscrupulous Elmer Gantrys is no excuse for our lack of preaching for and preparing for the response. Certainly the manipulation of an audience was known in Jesus' day. He did not allow that to stop him from preaching for a response, and neither should we.

CHAPTER FIVE

FORM—HOW WILL I SAY IT?

The primary reason unchurched Americans give for not going to church is that it is "boring." God save us from the culturally unpardonable sin of being boring. This has as much to do with how we say it as what we say. Many a fine sermon is lost on the congregation because the service and the sermon are disgustingly boring. What *form* will the sermon take?

We live in a culture that is comfortable with Bloomberg News TV. There are at least five things happening simultaneously on the screen when one watches the Bloomberg Report. Fox News, MS-NBC, and CNN have followed suit and offer several images and means of information at the same time. The people in our culture are expecting the communication they receive to be fast-paced, professionally produced, choreographed and planned to move in such a way as to keep their attention.

Into a culture such as this many churches and pastors are communicating the same way we did fifty years ago. Even some of our print publications such as our bulletins have changed little except for being produced on a photocopier rather than a mimeograph machine. Warren receives the weekly bulletin mailed from a church he served more than 25 years ago. The bulletin is unchanged. And the church is unchanged. Our music is the same as that of our parents and grandparents. Our order of worship is essentially the same as it was when Ozzie and Harriet were representative of American family life.

Since life as we know it has changed so much in the last fifty years, why has worship changed so little? The standard answer is that we proclaim timeless truths that are not subject to the trends of the time. If that were absolutely true we would still be speaking the gospel in Greek, Hebrew and Aramaic. We would still sing the psalms in Hebrew. We would still observe Jewish traditions.

No, the reason we have refused to change with the times is that change is uncomfortable and unpleasant for most of us. Those of us in the church have been unable to stop or slow the rapidity of change in our culture, so we have insisted on controlling it in our churches. There we have power over our lives and destinies (or so we think). Therefore we will not let anyone upset our world at church, not even for the sake of the gospel and the lost people in our communities. We will sing as we sang, we will worship as we worshiped, we will read as we read, we will do church as we have always done church and everyone else outside the church can just go to hell if they do not like it. And they will.

Our way of doing church is simply too boring to attract the unchurched. But since so many of us value our own comfort more than the salvation of the lost, we insist on maintaining our traditions. "It was good enough for my mother and father and it's good enough for me."

However, those who have read this far obviously desire to find a way to be effective in preaching and reaching the world with the gospel of Jesus Christ. You obviously believe that in Christ rests the only hope for life in this world and in the next. Therefore, you want to find effective ways to reach others with the good news.

THOU SHALT NOT BORE!

First of all, do not be boring! Whatever you do in worship, whatever you say in the sermon, do so with some enthusiasm and life. Keep the pace moving. Get rid of the dead spots in your worship service and in the delivery of your sermon. Move, move, move. For some this will mean moving out of the pulpit, if you are still using one. For some it will mean moving away from your manuscript. For others it will mean moving to the next sentence with all deliberate speed rather than in the plodding fashion of a previous generation's mentor.

If you are to avoid the deadly trap of being boring, you must understand what listeners are saying to you. Listen to them. They will tell you what they need and want. There are several things we have heard unchurched people of our culture saying to us. Maybe this is what they are trying to say to you if you are listening.

SPEAK TO ME

"Speak to my real or perceived needs. Talk about me. I don't really care what happened 2,000 or 4,000 or 50 years ago. Speak to my *sitz in leben*. Connect with my world. It doesn't matter what the gospel has to say unless it says it to me. And in order for that to happen it must engage me at some real point in my life. It must touch some hurt in my life. It must touch some hope in my life. If it doesn't touch me, then I am bored with the whole event."

Obviously a theologically trained author who is out of touch with the culture wrote some of that sermon. Who in our world would ever say *sitz in leben* other than someone with too many useless degrees? However, the unchurched would cry out for us to speak to their real situation in life.

A sermon dealing with sexual purity in today's world must speak to issues of celibacy in singleness and grace for those already living together out of marriage. In the real world, people of all ages are living together and are not married. In the real world, people are addicted to internet pornography and are going to nude bars for business lunches. In the real world, sexual standards are anything but clear and defined. Therefore, do not speak to sexual morality without speaking to these real issues, the real issues of life today.

SPEAK MY LANGUAGE

Have you ever attended a service where the entire service was conducted in a foreign language, a language you did not know? If you have, you know how boring and irrelevant the service is to you. You also know the joy of recognizing something you know, such as the Apostles' Creed, the Lord's Prayer, or a hymn. Worship conducted in a foreign language leaves the listener cold, uninvolved, and bored.

In the early 1990s Warren spent a week teaching in Latvia. This was not long after the fall of the Iron Curtain. He spoke in English, but every lesson was simultaneously translated into Russian and Latvian. Twice a day, the local hosts would lead the 250 attendees in worship. During worship they would sing several songs. Occasionally, they would sing a song that attending Americans recognized. Our faces lighted up and we sang at the top of our lungs. Finally, they were singing something we understood—at least we understood the tune and knew the meaning of the words.

The unchurched are saying, "Speak in words I know." What good does it do to work hard all week to prepare and deliver a sermon, then speak it in a language the general public cannot understand? One might as well walk into my world and begin preaching in Chinese. I simply could not understand it. We must speak the language of the culture.

How do we speak the language of the culture? We use words they understand. Secular culture does not know the meaning of our "church words," our "religious words," our "liturgical words." *Epiphany* has no meaning in our culture. *Stewardship* might have meaning in the context of a conversation with a representative of the Sierra Club, but it certainly has no religious significance in our culture. *Prophecy* is the province of Scientologist and science fiction writer L. Ron Hubbard and the Psychic Hot Line. It has no religious meaning. *Sovereignty* is about national sovereignty, not about God. *Grace* speaks to one's physical prowess and beautiful movement, not about God's unmerited love. *Sin* has no meaning of any kind in our secular culture, unless it is the sin of intolerance.

Many other words that contain essential meaning for the Gospel have no meaning in our culture. Therefore to use them without adequate translation is to speak a foreign language. Use words that help folks understand these concepts, and over time, they may understand the words. Start with the known and move to the unknown. This is the basis for any effective communication.

SPEAK TO ME, NOT ABOUT ME

"Do not speak in the third person. And talk to *me*. Can the canned sermons and illustrations. Speak to my life, to my hurts and hopes. Talk to me."

Effective preaching engages the listener by speaking directly and intimately to him or her. The preacher is not talking about hypothetical situations, not telling third-party stories picked up from some internet illustration service. The words of the sermon, the images painted by the words, the issues raised by the sermon are the words, images and issues of the listener's life.

Obviously this requires knowing who the listener is as well as what words, images and issues are familiar to him or her. Well-educated preachers do not always know the language of the people they are trying to reach. That is not necessarily because the target audience is uneducated. It may simply be because the target group is educated in a different language.

We have discovered that accountants and mainline preachers speak a different language. Neither one is very good at communicating with the other. Hence, often very little effective dialogue takes place.

The same may be true of preachers and musicians. One of the reasons for so many problems between preachers and musicians is because they speak different languages.

One might go so far as to say this is the case between men and women. It might even be possible to insinuate that men are from one planet and women are from another. Why? Because we speak different languages.

Effective communication and effective preaching require the preacher to speak the language of the hearer, or at least to provide adequate translation. Both of the authors have preached several times in a variety of foreign countries—Warren always with a translator and Dan now preaching in Spanish as well as English. The translator takes the unknown tongue of the preacher and translates it into the language of the listener.

Therefore, if today's preacher is going to speak in an unknown tongue and use a word like *redemption*, he or she must provide some kind of translation using words that the people of the culture do understand. This will bridge the gap between the known and the unknown and foster the possibility of effective communication. And effective communication is necessary for transformational preaching.

SPEAK TO ME, NOT THEM

"I am the one listening. Say something that will help me. I really don't care about the other 100 or 1,000 in the congregation. Make it personal for me; make it intimate for me."

Many a sermon has been preached to people who are not there to hear it. How often has a preacher attacked the evils that keep people from church? The listener who bothered to come that day only hears why others do not come and how very sinful they are for not coming. That listener leaves the service thinking, "What about me? I was here. Doesn't the Bible have something to say to me? I made the effort to be here. Speak to me, not 'them.' 'They' are not here to hear it anyway."

Effective preachers and effective sermons address the real felt needs of those who are in the worship service. A service made up primarily of seekers probably should not focus on the differences between premillennial, postmillennial and amillennial theology. A service designed primarily for mature Christians should not speak in great detail about the difference between Jesus and Rod Stewart.

A service targeting Gen-Xers probably should not use very many farming illustrations.

To speak to the people present requires envisioning who will be present as one is researching and writing the sermon. It requires thinking about how they speak and speaking to them in similar ways. Transformational preaching has the ability to get inside the head of the listener and speak in intimate and effective ways. Often the effective preacher will hear someone say, "I thought you were talking just to me today. It was as if you had read my email."

SPEAK AS IF YOU MEAN IT

"I do not care what you think. I do not care what others think or have thought before you. I want to know what *you* know. I want to know what you believe is worth dying for. I want to know what you believe with all your heart. Others' opinions do not matter if you are just quoting them. Tell me what you know to be true in your own life and experience."

Passionless preaching is anathema in the mission church. Yet why is it that some preachers sound as if they are selling burial plots at the local cemetery?

Effective preaching speaks *the language of the heart*—both the heart of the preacher and the heart of the listener. And its message emanates from the very heart of God.

Therefore, effective preachers, transformational preachers, are more at home with the Amoses and Jeremiahs and John the Baptists of this world than the chronicler and the scribe. They sound more like a NASCAR announcer than a professional golf analyst. They would be more at home at the ringside in Madison Square Garden at the fight of Lewis and Tyson than at the figure skating competition in the same location.

The effective preacher must burn with passion. The message must be fired by passion. The delivery must be aflame with passion if we expect the unchurched to come and hear the gospel. No amount of scholarly exegesis, trendy illustrations, crafty construction and silver-tongued oratory will overcome the lack of passion. The message must burn in the heart of the messenger. People must detect that fire.

Energy, passion, movement, and soul talk are the marks of the transformational preacher and sermon. Cold, lifeless and boring are the marks of the ineffective sermon.

SPEAK TO ME WITH YOUR EYES, NOT ONLY YOUR MOUTH

"Look at me when you talk to me. Make eye contact with me. Let your body communicate that you are talking to me, not someone else."

Have you ever had the unpleasant experience of running into someone in a crowd, striking up an conversation with him, and then observing the disconcerting way he talks to you, but is looking over your shoulder at someone else all the time? Of course you have. It makes you feel insignificant and unimportant, and it makes the person with whom you are in conversation appear uncaring and insensitive.

The same is true with preaching. An effective preacher will look into the eyes of the listener—even if he or she preaches from a manuscript! In the small church this is not a problem. The preacher can actually make eye contact with almost everyone in the congregation on any given Sunday.

What about the preacher who addresses several hundred or even several thousand every Sunday? How can he or she speak to each listener?

The effective preacher communicates in the large church in much the same way he or she would or did in the small church. The pastor picks out individuals in the various sections of the room and speaks to those persons, making eye contact and reading the response. By the preacher moving his attention around the room to actual individuals in the room and speaking to them, he is perceived to be speaking to everyone.

Occasionally a preacher may be in a setting so large that she cannot see everyone in the congregation. Again, speak to the section even if you cannot speak to the individual. Do not leave out the balcony or the back pews or the choir. Look at them. Speak to them. Folks will notice if you do this. They will also notice if you do not. But they will not notice it for long. They will be gone.

SPEAK CREATIVELY

"I want to hear something interesting, presented in an interesting fashion. Do not give me a lecture. Do not follow the same prescribed sermon format week after week."

Be willing to be interactive. This is not the day for pontification above and beyond the people. Interaction, authenticity, genuineness, intimacy, and transparency are what people are looking for today in a sermon and in a preacher.

Do not be afraid to carry on a conversation with someone in the congregation in the sermon—or a representative of the congregation. Do not be afraid even to let the listeners "overhear" the conversation within your own head about the text for the day. Open up to the creativity of the Creator as you create your sermon and the preaching experience.

Mike Brough was the pastor of Southland Christian Church in Lexington, Kentucky. He is also one of the finest preachers of this generation. When one of the authors attended worship there, Rev. Brough preached on the Sermon on the Mount. His thesis was that each point Jesus made in the sermon built on the previous point culminating in his admonition about persecution. The preacher made each point to be like the steps on a stepladder with the highest point being the top rung of the ladder. However, he did not just allude to a ladder or speak hypothetically. He had a stepladder in the chancel. It even had the right number of steps on it. Each time he made a new point from the Sermon on the Mount, he climbed up the ladder to the next step and spoke for a moment from that step before moving back down to be more on the level with the listener. His creativity caused this calloused listener of sermons to take notes and remember the gist of the message at least six years later.

Creativity is welcome in today's pulpit. Creativity is required in today's pulpit. Gimmicks are never appropriate. Climbing a ladder if one is afraid of heights is not appropriate. However, each and every preacher can be creative within the limits of his or her own gifts and personality. The reward will be that people will actually listen to the sermon and can even experience transformation through the power of the Gospel—once they hear it!

SPEAK TO ME WITH AUTHENTICITY

"Be yourself. Did God call you? Then I need to hear from you. Do not try to be someone you are not. I will see through it. Transparency and authenticity are what I am looking for in a preacher. If you are plastic, I am gone."

Several years ago one of the authors invited a friend to preach in his church. This preacher had a very high-pitched tenor voice and a thick Southern accent—a south Georgia Southern accent. But when he stepped into the pulpit he spoke with the voice of God in a Cecil B. DeMille production of *The Ten Commandments*! I was shocked! Where did this voice come from? Who was speaking in my pulpit? It certainly was not the preacher I had invited to preach. Neither I nor the rest of the people in the congregation really listened to him that day. It simply was not authentic.

I was listening to another preacher deliver a good sermon. The sermon built to a climax around the story of a mistake made in sharing a pack of cookies with a fellow traveler in an airport. It was a great story told in the first person. Imagine my disappointment in discovering the same story printed in a book by an author other than the preacher prior to the alleged event in the life of that preacher. I was never able to "hear" that preacher again with the same trust and enthusiasm.

We are preaching to very sophisticated audiences. They can find the same sermon material on the internet we can find. The pirating of stories and the dishonesty of making them our own will surely find us out—either in this life or the next. As a District Superintendent, Warren has had the unpleasant experience of hearing from congregations that they have caught their preachers stealing sermons from the internet. Their plagiarism, their lack of transparency and authenticity, cost them their effectiveness in their churches and the trust of their people. Transformational preaching comes from an authentic preacher proclaiming an authentic message in an authentic way that is true to who he or she is. Today's listener is looking for an authentic messenger.

SPEAK INTIMATELY WITH ME

"Tell me about you and talk with me about me; then I might be able to hear you talk with me about God. If you will not be intimate with me in your sermon, I will not trust you enough to hear what you want me to hear about Jesus. Experts and scholars and authorities can be important, but I want you to talk to me."

There was a time not very long ago when preachers were taught in the seminaries of America to avoid any first-person illustrations. We were to avoid ever speaking in the first person. Instead of saying what we thought, we were to speak in the third person. One might even say one should never speak of one's own feelings, life experiences, hurts, hope, aspirations, struggles, or longings. What bad advice!

Allen Hunt was being positioned to take over the senior minister role at a very large and complicated church, Mount Pisgah United Methodist Church in Alpharetta, Georgia. He would follow in the footsteps of Warren Lathem, a pastor who had been there for over 17 years and whose life had been very open to the congregation.

Just three years prior, the congregation had gone through the tragic deaths of their pastor's 20-year old son, Ray; their Hispanic minister, Carlos Gonzalez; and another couple from the church, Roger and Dana Lane. They were killed in the crash of ValuJet

Flight 592 from Miami to Atlanta while returning from a mission trip to Venezuela.

The church had practically raised Ray. They had seen him through childhood and adolescence and rebellion and college failure and his prodigal journey home and his preaching of his first of what promised to be many sermons. Not only that, but Warren Lathem had become the patriarch of the church, having outlived most others in the church. He had married many of them. Buried many of their loved ones. Baptized most of their children. He had been with them through sickness, tragedy, celebrations and joys. He had led them through the rapid changes required from being a church of 75 in worship with a budget of $75,000 to having more than 3,000 in worship and a budget of more than $10 million.

The new young minister had his work cut out for him. How could he possibly be as real and authentic as the old preacher? How could he possibly know as much about real life issues, struggles and problems?

So in one of Dr. Hunt's first sermons he told about when he and his young family were living in Connecticut and he was attending school at Yale. While there he was diagnosed with a horrible disease which resulted in very radical surgery. That was followed by the diagnosis of a skin melanoma. At the very time he was scheduled for surgery, his wife had a miscarriage and they wound up in a hospital together.

As he told these stories he did not create a picture of himself as a man of great faith or paint a self-portrait of a great hero. He spoke with brutal honesty and integrity of the struggle and the sufficiency of the grace of God in the midst of the struggle.

That was probably the most important sermon he preached in his first three years in that congregation. It let them know he was real. It let them know he was authentic. It let them know he too knew what it was to hurt, to be afraid, to be doubtful of the future. It also let them know he was a man of faith to whom God had given mercy, grace and insight into the human predicament.

Proper self-revelation is essential to effective preaching. Listeners want to know the preacher is personally invested in the message. They are not interested in theme papers or theological treatises. Today's listeners want a preacher to speak from his or her own heart and life experience. Only then can he or she speak to theirs. A quick word of caution is helpful here—the preacher should share personal experiences but not *private* experiences.[1]

SPEAK TO ME WITH DIVERSITY

"Please do not do the same thing every week. 'Three points and a poem' just will not be adequate in my world. Surely the gospel is too big to be wrapped in the same neat little 20-minute package every week."

Use a variety of forms in your preaching. Try using a recurring refrain on occasion (e.g., "You never know when you are going to need a shepherd.") Sometimes invite the congregation to speak the main point back to the preacher and to their neighbor. Preach an expository sermon one week and a topical sermon the next—or better yet, follow an expository series with a topical series. Try building the sermon around a "not this, but this" comparison and contrast model. Use three points one week and one point the next.

Predictability is corrosive, even lethal. People are used to cable TV and satellite dishes, Internet and personal digital organizers and iPods and Bluetooth technology. They want, they need, they expect lots of options, lots of variety. The effective, wise, transformational preacher will provide some of that in his or her preaching.

And when he or she does, the gospel will be proclaimed in a way the unchurched can hear it and lives will be changed. To fail to do so is to fail an entire generation in the proclamation of the gospel.

[1] Insight received from personal conversation with Dr. George Hunter.

CHAPTER SIX

TRANSFORMATIONAL WORSHIP—AN EXPERIENCE THAT LEADS TOWARD RESPONSE

It is clear that the sermon is the most critical tool for leading the worshiper toward a response to the gospel, and this book is intended primarily to help pastors learn to preach more effectively for a response. However, while the preacher and his or her sermon are the key elements in leading people to a response, the sermon does not take place in a vacuum. The rest of the worship experience is also critically helpful in moving people toward their personal response to the gospel.

So how do you get there? How do you begin to move toward the building of a comprehensive worship experience that provides people with flexible, transformational, integrity-based options for experiencing and responding to the gospel of Jesus Christ?

The central factors to consider are as follows:

SHAPING THE WHOLE SERVICE TO ENGENDER AN EXPERIENCE WITH THE GOSPEL

We hope you've gotten the picture concerning response. You understand the importance of offering the worshiper an accessible way to respond to the proclamation of the gospel. However, there is another aspect of worship/sermon planning that is critical to consider: How can we help the worshiper experience the gospel, in addition to responding to the gospel?

For example, if the theme of the worship service is healing, an important question to ask is: "How can the worshiper respond to the theme of healing at the conclusion of the worship experience?" But an equally important question is this: "How can the worshiper experience healing during the worship service, even before the response is issued?"

This way of thinking will require a quantum leap for many readers. We simply have not been trained to think in these ways. Perhaps you are the exception (praise God). If so, you may be thinking, "What's the big deal, don't most worship services help people experience the theme of the day?" The answer is, "They don't." Most worship services are not planned to help the worshiper experience peace, or experience forgiveness, or experience grace, or experience repentance during the worship service itself. In fact, it has been the experience of these authors that most worship services are not designed to follow a consistent theme of any kind; much less are they designed to help the worshiper experience something specific during the time of worship.

Both of us have consulted with dozens of churches, conducted scores of worship audits, mentored dozens of pastors and visited in hundreds of services both in person and via video analysis. As church after church has been visited through the years, it has been obvious that little advance planning and coordination has occurred. It has been obvious in most cases that the music team had no foreknowledge of what the preacher's sermon would be about, and the preacher had no foreknowledge of what the musical themes would be. Most worship services consist of individual pieces of which each has been designed in a vacuum and have no relationship to one another. In this setting, it truly takes a miracle of grace for a worshiper to experience transformation during the worship time.

So when a worship-planning team gets together, they must ask themselves (and God) at least these two questions:

What is the response we want to lead the worshiper toward?

How can we help the worshiper experience the theme of the day?

As these questions are addressed, the following factors can be considered:

- Congregational singing
- Presentational music
- Video testimonies
- Live testimonies
- Sermon
- Prayer (Pastoral prayer? Guided prayer? Praying for the person on one's right? Touch the person on the left as the pastor prays?)
- Response (Altar call? Pledge card? Registration card for a Bible study? Anointing? Baptism? Conversion? Communion? Healing?)
- Drama
- Video productions (different from testimony interviews)
- Movie clips
- The physical look of the worship space
- The look of the printed material
- Scripture (Read it? Act it out? Dance the Scripture? Have the congregation read it with the preacher?)
- Movement in the worship service
- Humor

As the worship team looks at these factors, and others that you will think of, the two-pronged goal must always be kept in mind: 1) to create an experience of the theme of the day, and 2) to lead the worshiper toward a specific, accessible, integrity-based response.

Accomplishing this will take creativity, prayer, insight, joy, and a heart that longs to see people transformed. It will require thinking of ways to make the gospel tangible in real-life, experiential ways.

These can be moments and opportunities for transformation of real people.

An example of this was observed in a worship service conducted by an esteemed colleague. It was a service of the renewal of the marriage vows. The entire worship service in this traditional congregation focused on the priority of the marriage covenant and the blessings that result from fidelity in marriage. After an excellent sermon a gifted soloist sang an appropriate song that extolled the blessings of a happy marriage and the grace evident in any marriage surrendered to Christ. Then couples exchanged the renewal vows. Individuals were invited to remember their marriage vows and give thanks, especially widows and widowers. Single adults were invited to give thanks for someone in their lives whose faithful marriage was a blessing to them. Healing words were spoken to those who had suffered the pains of a failed marriage. Very few left the service without having shed a tear in response to the gospel message and the function it performed in our midst. Our ability to respond in appropriate and comfortable ways made the service extremely meaningful.

Another example is seen in a recent healing service. The congregational singing, the choral singing, the prayers, and the sermon all focused on the theme of healing. Following the sermon, an invitation was given for people to come forward and be anointed with oil for healing, with a pastor simply saying the words, "Be healed in the name of Christ." Importantly, the invitation was not limited to those in need of physical healing. It also included those who could benefit from spiritual healing, financial healing, emotional healing, and relational healing. Additionally, people were invited to remain in their seats and pray quietly for those around them if they did not want to be anointed.

Designing the worship experience in this fashion gave the congregant many ways of experiencing the theme of healing throughout the service, and it also gave the congregant a great deal of flexibility in how he or she could respond to the offer of God's healing power in their lives. They could choose to be anointed or they could choose to remain seated. If they chose to remain seated, they could sing familiar worship choruses that were being played in the background, or they could pray. Upon choosing anointing, they could choose for which "type" of healing they were being anointed. The pastor's invitation made it clear that there was no specific expectation of their going forward. Yet, 99% of the congregation did go forward, with many people shedding tears of joy and gratitude as they experienced a powerful movement of the Holy Spirit.

A third example is seen in a recent Renewal of Baptism service. Again, flexibility and integrity were the key elements of leading people to a response. Following the sermon, the congregant was invited to come forward and have a pastor anoint his or her forehead with water in the sign of the cross, with the pastor saying "Remember your baptism, and be thankful." A separate invitation was given for those who had never received baptism and wanted to do so. This dual invitation allowed those who were already Christians to respond to the gospel that day by remembering God's grace in their lives and expressing gratitude for that grace. It also allowed those who were not already Christians to receive Jesus' forgiveness and begin a transformational relationship with Him. Approximately 95% of the congregation responded to one of these two invitations.

GROWING A RESPONSIVE CONGREGATION

We would like to offer another helpful insight: You must be intentional in growing a responsive congregation. Preaching for response and planning worship services that help people experience the gospel will be much more productive if the congregation is filled with people who are ready to respond. But if your congregation has seldom or never been asked to respond to the gospel, it will be unfair to expect their non-responsive mindset to be changed overnight. After all, they do not know differently. If you and previous pastors of your congregation have not been leading them to respond to the gospel in the context of the worship service, then it will feel very foreign to them when you start offering them opportunities for response. You will want to work with them patiently and lovingly as you grow together in this important aspect of your transformational worship life. You can begin to grow a responsive congregation in four primary ways.

1. Build response into the sermon itself (not simply at the end of the sermon).
2. Consistently ask them to respond.
3. Model response for them.
4. Make it as simple, easy, and clear as possible.

GROWING A RESPONSIVE CONGREGATION—BUILD RESPONSE INTO THE SERMON ITSELF

This is a simple but effective way to increase the overall responsiveness of your congregation. You will want to be judicious in how you do this so that the overall movement of your sermon is not derailed. But used in a well-balanced manner, the worshipers will begin to grow in their willingness to respond.

Examples include:

Occasionally say something like: "Turn to your neighbor and say 'God loves you just as you are.'"

Have them read the Scripture passage aloud with you.

Invite them to respond to you with a statement related to your sermon:

a) Preacher: "When all the jars have run out..."
   Congregation: "...the oil stops flowing."
b) Preacher: "God is good."
   Congregation: "All the time."

c) Preacher: "The love of Jesus..."
Congregation: "... is for everyone."

Invite them to raise a hand or stand up in response to a sermon point: "If you've ever experienced Christ as a loving Shepherd, please raise your hand."

Invite them to take notes.

If you want them to follow along in their Order of Worship as you read the Scripture, say something like: "I invite you to follow along as I read our Scripture passage this morning. [Pause a couple of seconds] If you're ready, say, 'Amen.'"

Invite them to sing something "off the cuff" with you, such as "Jesus Loves Me," or "I Am the Church," or "This Little Light of Mine."

If you've said something that was really important and helpful, in a humorous, humble tone of voice, say "Somebody oughta say, 'Amen.'"

Once you try this a time or two, you'll see the effectiveness of it, and you'll also think of even better ways to utilize this concept. This is the quickest way for the preacher to begin building a responsive congregation because the preacher can craft these ideas into the sermon as the sermon is being prepared. The preacher does not need to depend on anyone else to implement this idea.

GROWING A RESPONSIVE CONGREGATION—CONSISTENTLY ASK THE CONGREGATION TO RESPOND.

This point is so basic that people often overlook it. If you're going to build a responsive congregation, then you need to ask them to respond on a consistent basis. Don't save your response invitations for Evangelism Sunday or Membership Sunday or the revival sermon. Invite your congregation to respond often, and invite them to respond in a variety of ways.

- Have an altar call (even these can be varied).
- Have a response card they can fill out to sign up for a group or class.
- Offer Communion and/or foot-washing.
- Invite them to be anointed with oil.
- Have them read a corporate prayer together.
- Ask them to give a special offering to help homeless people.
- Have a bulletin insert with a Scripture reading and a short prayer for each day of the following week.

The possibilities are myriad. Have fun thinking of different options. God will bless your creativity.

GROWING A RESPONSIVE CONGREGATION—MODEL RESPONSE FOR THEM

Another important component of growing a responsive congregation is that of helping the congregation observe the worship leaders/musicians/preachers as they participate in response. For example, help the choir feel free to clap when they feel like it. This gives the congregation "permission" to clap if they want to. Another example: If a worship leader is touched by a testimony or a song or a sermon illustration, he must be transparent enough to let the congregation see that he or she is touched. Does your congregation ever see a minister or worship leader or choir member or usher (heaven forbid!) kneel in prayer as a response to something in the worship experience? Do they see these people smile? Laugh? Cry? Raise their hands? Stand up? Read Scripture? Give?

The worship leaders have a wonderful opportunity to lead the congregation in this way. If the "up-front" folks never do anything but sit with a straight back and a somber face, that's the kind of congregation you will have. Please understand that the intent here is not to engender a carnival atmosphere. However, the intent is to engender an atmosphere of warmth and love and sharing and communication and joy and response. You have enormous potential to influence your congregation in this way. Take advantage of this opportunity. A lost person's eternal destiny will eventually weigh in the balance, because the more your congregation becomes used to seeing response the more comfortable they will become in responding themselves.

GROWING A RESPONSIVE CONGREGATION—MAKE IT SIMPLE, EASY, AND CLEAR

This is fairly self-explanatory. Simply put: you *do* want to include response in a variety of ways, but don't let the variety lead you to make the responses complicated. Make them clear and simple.

CHAPTER SEVEN

PREPARING FOR TRANSFORMATIONAL WORSHIP—PLANNING AHEAD

One of the most inhibiting factors to offering worship and preaching for the kind of response that will result in transformed lives is the failure to plan adequately far enough in advance. Creative, dynamic worship requires time for planning, recruiting, rehearsing, and prayer. Effective preaching requires time for the concepts to germinate in the mind and heart of the preacher. Carefully thought-out response demands planning in order to implement the most effective response possibilities.

Effective preachers typically will know what they will be preaching at least three months in advance, and sometimes as much as a year or 18 months. Why? Nothing great is ever built without planning.

One church where these authors have served has recently constructed a $20 million, 3,000 seat sanctuary. It took 18 months to build. However, it took 18 months previous to that to design. But before it could be designed, money had to be raised to ensure it could actually be built. It took a year to raise the money. But before the money could be raised, land had to be purchased. That also took a year. Before land could be purchased someone had to have the vision and share that vision with the leadership and the entire congregation. That took half a year. While it took 18 months to build this 100,000 square feet building, planning for it began five and a half years before.

It is a great structure and a wonderful tool for ministry, but it would never have come into being without adequate planning and adequate time for planning. Many people had to be brought into the circle of planning before such a great edifice resulted.

HOW DO YOU PLAN WORSHIP?

It begins in the heart of the preacher. The preacher must find time to get away from the routine of the church and discover the texts, themes, subjects and needs he or she will want to address. Some people do this best when absolutely alone.

However, we have found it to be good to do this in the company of another preacher. The two can brainstorm, pray, discern and discover the ways God is leading in the preaching.

Therefore, pick a date to get out of the office, preferably a couple of days in a retreat setting. The two or three preachers get together with the church year laid out before them. This includes both the liturgical year and the local church year. For example, it doesn't matter if Pentecost Sunday is the first Sunday in June in one church this author knows of. That is the day the church does the big barbeque at the huge community fair. Pentecost can wait until the next Sunday in that church. Pigs need to be roasted. But Pentecost needs to come as well.

PLAN THE CALENDAR

This really has to be done before the worship themes or sermons can be planned. When is the annual giving campaign? That has to be included in the planning mix. Is there a Sunday devoted to raising support for building a Habitat house? Is there a special Sunday with an emphasis on children's ministry? Are the youth going to be conducting the worship service one Sunday? What about Laity Sunday? What about the Sundays the preacher will be on vacation?

Therefore, it is easy to see why planning the calendar is a prerequisite to planning the worship themes. To plan a worship theme on "Aging with Grace" on the Sunday the youth are leading worship will not result in a very effective worship experience in most churches.

Of course, effective calendar planning that results in a comprehensive approach to congregational life development is an art unto itself and beyond the scope of this book. We simply assume the reader will know how to plan the church calendar at least 18 months in advance. Effective worship planning presupposes effective all-church calendar planning – at least as it relates to worship.

PLAN THE THEMES

Once the calendar is planned and you are away, you are ready to plan the worship themes. Pick a date to begin. For instance if you go away for this purpose in January, begin planning for Sundays no earlier than March, preferably April. Everyone needs at least three months lead time to prepare for the planned service; anything less than that will result in a less than stellar experience.

In most churches in America Mother's Day is celebrated on the second Sunday in May. That is a good day to speak to issues of the Christian home, parenting, families, etc. So if the preacher feels God is leading him or her to speak to some particular issue related to one of these areas, Mother's Day might be a good time to do so.

Given the special days and holidays, at least some themes must be addressed each year. These merit attention because of the necessity for growth and development of the church and the spiritual maturity of the congregation.

EVANGELISM

One of the richest fields for evangelism in America is Sunday morning in our worship services. This is true both for congregations that are reaching the unchurched and those made up of mostly church folks.

Evangelism Sundays acknowledge the truth that in any congregation some people have never made a personal response to the claims of Christ. People of all ages simply have never accepted the benefits of grace offered in Jesus Christ.

By focusing on evangelism at least one Sunday each year (we advise more than one), our folks are given an opportunity to make a personal faith commitment to Christ. The whole service is planned around this theme and the response is carefully designed to make a response a very natural result for one who is unsaved. Obviously, this means that we believe in salvation in and through Jesus Christ, "for by grace are you saved through faith . . . ."

MISSION/OUTREACH

Every church defines mission and outreach in its own specific terms. For us, mission is what occurs in the name of Christ outside our city. Outreach is what we do inside the city. Mission is "foreign," e.g., beyond our own community, and outreach is local.

However, whether it is local or foreign, every Christian needs to be invited to participate in mission outreach. Service is a part of Christian growth and a proper response to grace. Active participation in mission is a transformational experience both for those served, but also for those serving.

So at least once a year, preferably more often, we design worship theme(s) around the mission of the church, and the expected response is to volunteer to engage in mission. This may be an invitation to prepare Meals on Wheels for shut-ins on holidays or an extended time building a church in Venezuela. However, the theme is always developed in such a way as to invite individual participation in the mission.

GIVING DEVELOPMENT

Jesus said, "Where your treasure is, there will your heart be also." The modern church has reversed the order of Jesus' words and said, "Get a person's heart right, and the money will take care of itself." Nothing could be further from the truth. Jesus "knew what was in man [and woman]." He knows our hearts.

Growth in giving is a means of grace to growth in discipleship. Every year one to three services must lift up the biblical message of giving. These services will invite listeners to make a response to biblical standards and make a commitment of their own giving.

Certainly if Jesus said more about the proper use of money (according to the Gospels) than he did about prayer, we also ought to give it significant attention. Certainly the church will benefit from this thematic approach to giving. But far more importantly, the individual giver will discover a means of grace he or she never knew existed.

CARING

Themes that are consistent with the areas of emphasis in the ministry of Jesus build up the church. From the very earliest evidence of the ministry of Jesus in the synagogue in Capernaum to his dealings with the repentant thief on the cross, Jesus cared for the needs of people. As Matthew says in 9:35, Jesus went about teaching, preaching and healing.

This emphasis on caring is consistent with the emphasis of Jesus on healing. Just as he cared for the poor, the disenfranchised, the sick, the broken and the grieving, so are we to become active caregivers. Worship services focused on caring can include a Call to Care Sunday in which the congregation is invited to volunteer for a significant ministry of caring. Develop a model similar to Frazer Memorial United Methodist Church's *Every Member in Ministry*, by John Ed Mathison.

Congregations are unforgiving places when adequate caring is not demonstrated within the congregation. The lack of caring is a great "dis-satisfier" in any congregation. A certain level of pastoral care must be provided by the clergy staff. However, neither the budget nor the distribution of spiritual gifts allows for caring to be the exclusive work of the clergy. The congregation must be cared for also by caring members of the congregation. Stephen Ministry creates a great model for this to occur.

PRAYER

It was the custom of Jesus to spend much time in prayer. Spiritual giants do not develop apart from serious devotion to prayer. Great churches do not develop without a serious devotion to prayer within the congregation.

At least yearly the church should have a Sunday devoted to the ministry of prayer. People need to pray. People need someone to pray for them. And the church needs prayer warriors regularly engaged in prayer.

Every Sunday will include a prayer time, will have opportunity for prayer requests, will encourage praying for one another and the community and the needs of the world. But at least once a year the effective preacher will focus solely on prayer and invite the congregation to respond to the opportunity to pray. The church will be built up by its emphasis on prayer. Many great things will never be considered without a high value placed on prayer.

VISION

The preacher is the primary "vision-caster" in any congregation. He or she must work constantly on putting the vision before the congregation in a great variety of settings. One of the most important settings for doing this is the primary worship service(s). Many, perhaps most, of the people we reach will only be involved in worship. They will probably not go to Sunday school. They will probably not be involved in small groups. They will probably not serve on a committee or come to a Wednesday night dinner. They come to worship only.

If they are going to have any opportunity at all to understand and embrace the vision of the church, that opportunity must come in and through worship. Therefore, at least yearly the worship theme needs to be built around God's preferred future for that congregation.

DISCIPLESHIP

Effective congregations have a method, a process, for the development of discipleship. Ours was called The Mount Pisgah Experience. At least once a year we focused on the need for "going on to perfection," to use a good Wesleyan term from our heritage. This growth in grace, this developing into the full stature of Christ, this Deeper Life, is essential if a congregation is to experience spiritual growth and development.

Therefore at least once a year the theme of worship must focus on discipleship. The entire service, including the sermon and response is designed to help the congregant become engaged in some process of personal spiritual growth. Since this seems most often to take place in small groups, this will often be a time to lift up the small group ministry of the church. Then we recruit for these small groups as a means of encouraging growth in grace.

Every reader will have at least one area he or she feels must be included every year. Great! Include that in your list of themes that have to be addressed annually. The mission field where you serve will dictate themes peculiar to your context for ministry.

There are other themes we will want to address in worship. Easter should be included in our thematic worship planning. We would not want to leave out Advent and Christmas. Lent deserves attention. The sacraments merit our emphasis.

In planning the themes for each Sunday of the year, it will quickly become evident that 52 Sundays simply are not enough. Therefore, we are forced to carefully plan the themes we will address and do so on the appropriate Sundays.

PLAN THE TEXTS, SERMON THEMES, AND TITLES

You now have your calendar before you, and it includes the theme to be addressed on each Sunday of the period you are planning. Now is when the residual of your personal Bible study, devotional reading and general knowledge of Scriptures bears the most fruit.

Look at the theme and begin to consider what texts might speak to that theme.

For instance, the Sunday you focus on caring, the text about the maniac of Gedera might work. Or what about the feeding of the 5,000? Or would a text from Amos be more appropriate?

Prayerful discernment is needed here. I also like to have someone with me on whom I can bounce off ideas about text as we look at it together. Then we will choose the one to become the foundation for the preaching that day.

Once we have decided on a text, the next step is to determine the Scripture theme (related to the theme for the day) that becomes our focus in worship. Perhaps on Caring Sunday, the text we choose is Luke's account of the feeding of the 5,000. The Scripture theme that may develop is the sharing of what we have with those in need, with particular focus on how God blesses what we give to others. This might be stated as succinctly as "God blesses when we give to someone in need."

Now that we have the Scripture text and theme, we move to the title of the sermon. Any number of ideas may come to mind: "Food for One, Food for All," "How Much Do You Have?" "Is that All You Have?" "Can Jesus Bless That?" Several others might pop up in the brainstorming. One will be right.

Choose the name of the sermon that the Spirit impresses on you, list it with the Scripture text, the theme of the text and the worship theme for the day. Do this for each Sunday in the planning period. Then you will have completed your work for this time away. Then you can go fishing!

PLAN THE WORSHIP

Upon returning from your planning time, clean up your work and put it into a document that can be distributed to everyone who will be involved in worship planning. Give them time to look it over. Then gather the group for the planning of at least two months of worship services, beginning at least two months in the future.

Who needs to be involved in this process? That will depend entirely on the church and the size of the congregation and staff. In a very large church this group might be as large as six or eight people. In a small church it may be only three. In either case, laity ought to be included.

Meet in someone's living room or retreat center close to the church, but far enough away to avoid interruptions. Once everyone is comfortable and in possession of coffee or water or Coca Cola, have a time of prayer. Then with one person recording the proceedings on a computer or on paper, begin with the first Sunday under consideration. The work begins with a discussion of the theme, the scripture, the scripture theme, and the title. This gets everyone thinking along the same lines. It starts the creative juices flowing and gives opportunity for the Holy Spirit to work among us.

Here is a good time for everyone present to help write the sermon. Each person is welcome to make comments about how to approach the sermon, offer any good ideas for the sermon and specifically suggest what kind of response should be invited and how it should be invited.

A good portable white board and erasable markers will make this move quickly. Newsprint will also work. On the board or newsprint plan the order of worship assigning times allotted for each facet of the service. As you go through the service discuss each part. This is not the time to plan every piece of music or write the pastoral prayer. This is the time to plan with a broad stroke. The planning might look like this:

4 (minutes) Opening hymn or music set – praise and exciting
2 Welcome—pastor announces Marriage Renewal Retreat
5 Music set—led by men's group
1 Affirmation of faith
4 New members and baptism
3 Pastoral prayer

3 Video testimony—a couple who've been happily married for 35 to 50 years
4 Offering
4 Special music – maybe "Find Us Faithful"
20 Scripture reading and sermon ("The Seven-Year Itch")
6 Invitation (invite all married for fewer than seven years to the front for a consecration of their marriage; give each of them the Bede booklet on marriage)
1 Benediction
57 Total minutes

This type of planning can be done for eight or ten Sundays in one full day. However, it will be a long day. It gets harder after lunch. An early start and an early finish seem to work better. This is so intense that fatigue is a real danger to creativity.

For this to work well every person present must feel that what he or she contributes is valued. One person has to make the ultimate decision; that will be the senior minister or the preacher of the day. However, all input is valued and each person is esteemed for his or her unique contribution to the process.

The record of the day's planning is immediately "cleaned up" by the person who took the notes and distributed the next day by paper copy or electronically. The distribution list includes everyone who was present for the planning as well as anyone affected by it.

Each area of ministry then uses this document as the basis for their detailed planning. The music director selects all the music to support the theme and the purpose of the service. Any music that must be purchased is ordered and rehearsals begin. The video department (or contractor) conducts the interview with the pre-selected couple. Editing begins. The draft is shown to the worship team at least a week before its use. Final editing then follows. Bede booklets are ordered and the method of distribution worked out in detail. Detailed orders of worship are prepared and bulletin drafts are produced at least three weeks in advance. Others who must plan do so based on this planned order of worship.

This planning provides the framework in which staff and volunteers can do their best and most creative work. It is not restrictive. In fact, it is just the opposite. It fosters creativity and ownership of the worship experience by more than one person. It will result in vastly improved services in most churches.

DETAIL THE WORSHIP

Every week the worship team meets on Monday or Tuesday. It reviews first the bulletin and order of worship for the coming Sunday. Every detail is looked at and final proofing is completed. Any last minute changes necessitated by unexpected circumstances are made at this time.

Then copies of the bulletin draft of the service (two weeks in advance) are distributed. The same process is followed with the next Sunday's bulletin. The primary difference is we have enough time to make some significant changes and improvements as necessary.

Finally, copies of the draft of the order of worship are distributed three weeks hence. At this point wholesale changes are possible if it has become necessary. Perhaps a special need in the community has risen since we planned worship. We can decide in this session to change the theme completely and address the new need. This requires us to go back to the same process we had used some weeks earlier and repeat the process around the newly presented opportunity and theme.

EDIT THE WORSHIP

This is done each week by someone on the worship team. The camera-ready copy of the bulletin or order of worship is in hand just before it is to go to print. If only PowerPoint is used and no printed material is used, it also goes to this person for proofing. He or she signs off on the worship document, it gets produced and is used in worship.

Some would think this an unnecessary step given all the attention to this in weekly meetings. That is a false assumption. All of us make mistakes. And anything that can go wrong with an order of worship will. This step is critical. It needs to be done by the member of the worship team who has the best eye for detail. Avoid embarrassing errors.

When Warren served a small congregation, he came into the sanctuary of the church not long before worship was to start. The secretary had produced the bulletin and placed the hundred or so printed copies on the table in the narthex and one copy on the pastor's desk. Warren looked at the announcement that asked people to supply the names and contact information for anyone in the community who was shut in. Only the secretary had made a typo—the word *shut* was spelled with an *i* instead of a *u*. Fortunately, she had caught her own mistake late Saturday night and very early Sunday morning rescued the spoiled bulletins and replaced them with the correct ones—all except for the one on the pastor's desk!

Attention to detail and obsessive proofing are essential. Many have been doomed by this failure. A quick examination of some of the mistakes made in bulletins will prove this point without much debate.

EVALUATE THE WORSHIP

Each week when the worship teams gather, before bulletins are distributed and proofing begins, before any discussion of next week's service ensues, we reflect. We evaluate the previous Sunday's service. Often, this is primarily a time of thanksgiving. If we have done our work well and God blessed our efforts, we have much for which to be grateful. Someone may tell about a decision a particular church member made as a result of the worship service. Another might repeat a comment over heard in the hallway between services. Someone else might simply tell the associate minister how much his pastoral prayer meant that day.

We also spend time evaluating why something did not turn out the way we had hoped. Who "dropped the ball?" Why? When? What could we have done differently? How can we avoid this same mistake again? What remedial action needs to be taken? This is not a time for picking at nits or pointing fingers. This is a time to explore carefully what needs to change for the sake of the gospel of Jesus Christ.

After all, what we do and what we say, how we preach and how we plan, what we sing and where we move, how we invite and how we respond are all for the glory of God in Jesus Christ. His gospel demands a response. May we do the very best we can to proclaim it with the power of the Holy Spirit, using the very best of our intellect and persuasive powers. And may our congregations be helped to respond to the gospel. This will make all the difference in the world—and the world to come.

CHAPTER EIGHT

PREPARING THE PREACHER

CONVERSION

There is no preacher before the transforming power of Christ enters the human heart. A preacher has an experience of conversion, of repentance of sin, of grace and of faith in Christ. An effective preacher will be able to recall clearly the power of conversion in his or her life and share the miracle of saving grace as a personal witness to the love and goodness of God.

Every preacher of historical note reflected upon his or her experience of grace and its transforming power in his or her life. This witness of saving grace provides the motivation to share the good news of Christ. This is why the world's most famous hymn says, "I once was lost, but now I'm found, 'Was blind but now I see."

A changed life has the authenticity needed to call others to this experience of grace. It provides the fundamental connection with all of "Adam's race." The preacher and the listener both begin with the universal need for salvation in Christ. Here they are one. This awareness of sin, grace and salvation is what binds the heart of the preacher to the heart of the listener.

PREVENIENT GRACE

An effective preacher will have reflected enough on his or her life to be able to declare much of how and when God's grace was poured out on that life: "While we were yet sinners, Christ died for us." This prevenient grace, the grace that goes before, is that which awakens within us the awareness of our need of a Savior and the desire to know Him. Effective preaching recognizes the influence of Christian witnesses, Christian parents and grandparents, loving pastors, faithful teachers, Christian coaches, and others who were a means of prevenient grace in the preacher's life. It also recognizes the influence of TV, books, computers, tracts, billboards and especially the Bible in bringing one to faith in Christ.

This awareness of prevenient grace keeps the preacher from beginning to think that he or she is responsible for the faith of others. All are solely responsible for their salvation. It calls the reflective heart to acknowledge its own depravity, the power of the influence of others under the anointing of the Holy Spirit and the majesty of grace—unmerited and undeserved love.

This is a good inoculation against the spiritual snobbery to which clergy are so prone. Every preacher will be well served to remember all the ways God has reached out to him or her. Spiritual superiority is an ugly thing and inhibits the spread of the gospel.

CALL

There is no effective preaching apart from a clear call. Every preacher of note in every generation testified to his or her sense of call. It is the awareness that God has said, "I have a purpose for your life. Your purpose in life is to preach the gospel. Will you live your life for the purpose for which I created you?"

Effective preachers are clear about their call. Without it they would be doing something else. But with it they have the great obsession of those called to God's work.

All of that means the preacher can be susceptible to arrogance. Since he or she is so sure of his call and since "God called me" is at the center of one's self-understanding, the effective preacher discovers a humility that saves him or her from spiritual arrogance. They are more amazed than anyone that God would call them and that God could use them.

However, that amazement does not negate the clear and sure awareness of God's call. It is that assurance that will be so important when the times get tough—and they will get tough for every preacher of the gospel of Jesus Christ.

SURRENDER

Surrender to the call is necessary for effectiveness in the call. The call to preach must become the "magnificent obsession" of the preacher's life. Other aspects of ministry and other attractions and opportunities take a backseat to the surrender to the call to preach. The great danger for the preacher is to devote time to many other good things and fail to devote adequate time and attention to the great thing: preaching. The tyranny of the urgent must never be allowed to subvert the necessity of the truly important.

Preaching is the most important activity of the preacher's life. Surrender to the call to preach is the surrender to a single-mindedness and a clarity of purpose that will guide the focus, time and energy of the preacher's life.

DEVOTIONAL LIFE

Great preaching springs from the deep wells of the soul. Those wells are dug in the solitude of prayer, praise and study conducted by the preacher in the lonely place with God. Busyness is the great threat to helpful preaching as it will subvert the daily walk an excellent preacher must maintain. This daily of devotional time with God will provide the preacher with the spiritual resources necessary to wage war on the principalities and powers that oppose the effective proclamation of the Word of God.

HOLINESS

Purity of mind and heart is necessary for the effectiveness of the pure gospel. Holiness of heart and life is necessary for effective preaching for response. Effective preachers will guard their moral, ethical and spiritual lives. Sin is the enemy of great preaching. Unconfessed and unrepentant sin in the life of a preacher will negate the effectiveness of the preaching. The effective preacher will engage in a process of self-examination of conscience that will result in purity of spirit necessary for transformational preaching. The preacher must be transformed by the power of the Holy Spirit for the power of the Holy Spirit fully to work through him or her for the redemption of the world. Holiness of heart and life is a prerequisite for preaching that glorifies Christ.

INTEGRITY

A lapse of integrity has ruined more preachers than all the mean and spiteful work of unregenerate church folk. Integrity of word and practice is essential for effective preaching. What we do speaks so loudly that what we say can be lost in a world hungry for integrity from its leaders. It is not enough genuinely to believe what we say in the pulpits of the church, but we must live it on the streets of the world. Preachers who desire to glorify Christ through their preaching will be especially sensitive to the maintenance of personal as well as professional integrity.

WORK ETHIC

"If it was easy, anyone could do it," has often been said about preaching. It is hard work, harder than any other work ever attempted by us—and that includes cleaning out chicken houses! Sloppy work habits result in sloppy results. Since many effective preachers are natural extroverts, the long hours spent alone in devotion and preparation represent hard work. Yet nothing will take the place of a good work ethic. This work ethic will compensate for smaller gifts and lesser lights. Similarly, without a strong work ethic, the most naturally or even super-naturally gifted preacher will settle into a repetitious pattern of preaching and preparation that results in less-than-stellar accomplishments for the kingdom.

While the old homiletical rule of thumb of one hour of preparation for every minute preaching may be an exaggeration, it is not far off the mark. It is certainly closer to the truth of the amount of work required for excellent preaching than what most preachers are willing to do. Certainly, the personal preferences and work habits of individual preachers will vary. Some will invest considerable time in sermon preparation every week. Others will invest whole days monthly or bi-monthly just working on sermons and will then spend 10 hours or less weekly.

However, no matter the individual work pattern, nothing takes the place of hard, hard work. Too few are willing to devote the tremendous amount of time and energy necessary to produce the best preaching of which we are capable. And nothing will take its place. Study, reflection, writing, rewriting, planning, searching, and wordsmithing are plain hard work. However, they are not so difficult as a cross, and must be practiced if the preacher is to reach his or her preaching potential.

TRANSPARENCY

Preaching that results in transformed lives emanates from a transformed life. How can the listener know the preacher has experienced the transforming power of the gospel? The preacher must live a life of transparency. Preaching is no place for role-playing. Why is it that so many ineffective preachers take on a "preacher voice" in the pulpit? Outside the pulpit they sound like Gomer Pyle speaking to Sergeant Carter. Inside the pulpit they sound like Gomer Pyle singing before the President! Today's listener is too sophisticated to be taken in by plastic preachers. They must be given windows to look into the life of the preacher if they are to be able to determine if the preacher really believes what he or she is saying. Mimicry and false veneers will expose the lack of soundness in the preacher. Preachers must be "what you see is what you get" if listeners are to really accept what preachers have to say.

ACCOUNTABILITY

Preaching can be the loneliest profession in the world. It can also be the profession with the least accountability. Therefore, preachers who desire to maximize their effectiveness will establish clear channels of accountability. This can be with other clergy, laity, or a group of peers, but effective preaching demands accountability.

This means a preacher who desires to reach his or her potential for Christ must submit to the authority of others. He or she must be open and communicative, honest and humble. Preachers must listen to what the Spirit is saying through others as well as to themselves. Effective preachers should establish an accountability group where their preaching is reflected upon, and perhaps more importantly, their lives.

MENTORING

The best preachers can name their mentors. This is the person (or persons) who modeled preaching for us. We listen, we learn, we copy, we emulate and we allow them to live through us. This is not to say that we become cheap carbon copies of an effective preacher. It is to say we value effective role models for us. We seek them out. We learn from them. And we are better at what we do because of them. All of this means we must have a teachable spirit.

TEACHABLE

"When the student is ready the teacher will appear," said an ancient philosopher. Excellent preachers are students of great preaching. They enjoy hearing great sermons. They listen to learn, to worship, to grow, not to criticize and dissect. Certainly criticism and dissection are useful learning tools and they have their place in the toolbox of preaching.

But far more important is the active listening to the messengers God sends our way to show us a better way of doing what we are called to do. Many of these will not be other preachers. Some will be insightful laity who will share honest reflection with us concerning our preaching. Others will be mentors and consultants and professors. Still others may be those we would least suspect of having anything helpful to say to us. But if we have a teachable spirit we can learn from anyone—and we will. For the Spirit is not limited to speaking only through credentialed individuals. One time the Holy Spirit spoke through Balaam's donkey.

A teachable student of preaching will listen to the lesson no matter what medium God may use to speak the truth to us. If we do not maintain a teachable spirit, nothing will get past the censors of our minds, the filters of our hearts. But if we are teachable, we will be amazed whom God will send our way to tell us what God wants us to know in order to proclaim with power and effectiveness the gospel of Jesus Christ.

CHAPTER NINE

12 KEYS TO EFFECTIVE PREACHING

Effective gospel preaching is always more dependent on substance than style. However, style is important. The technique one employs in delivering a sermon can enhance or detract from the substance. Hence, what are some techniques that enhance a sermon and facilitate the listener being more likely to respond positively to the gospel?

Many of these will seem overly simple or even trite to the experienced public speaker. However, after many years of teaching preaching, coaching young preachers and listening to hundreds, even thousands of sermons, the need to address these techniques is self-evident.

An esteemed professor of Christian worship was addressing his class at one of the most prestigious seminaries in the country. He began the class with this question: "What is the very last thing a preacher should do before stepping into the sanctuary to lead worship?"

A variety of responses were given, most of which sounded very pious. "Pray" was the most popular response. However, "Look over the sermon one last time" ran a close second.

When everyone who wanted to comment had done so, the professor proceeded to declare: "The very last thing a preacher should do before entering the sanctuary to lead worship is check his fly" (this was an all male class in a different age).

After the laughter died away a couple of students were horrified that this esteemed professor of Christian worship should make such a trite and mundane statement. Imprudently, they expressed their displeasure. To which the old professor replied, "Do you really think anyone is going to take you seriously when you are preaching with your fly open?"

The point was well made. No amount of skillful sermon crafting and poignant delivery can overcome such an obstacle. The wise old professor prevailed.

Many average sermons could be heard by the congregation as being above average if the preacher would simply pay attention to some simple, yet absolutely necessary, details. The lack of attention to these very simple details will cause a congregation to disengage from hearing the message and will lead to criticism of the preacher.

Several years ago a particular preacher was on TV every Sunday. His sermons were well crafted and theologically sound. However, he was so very difficult to listen to that these well-crafted sermons evidencing a great deal of preparation and concern were heard as mediocre or poor. One of these authors often remarked to his wife upon hearing one of these sermons, "I wish he would just write the sermon and let me preach it!" The TV preacher never made much of an impact in 40 years of ministry because, at least in part, his preaching and speaking techniques were simply so inferior. No one could really hear what he had to say because the way he said it was so poor.

So what are these miracle techniques that will result in vastly improved preaching grades on Sunday? They are not miracle techniques. But they do matter.

KEY NUMBER 1—ENUNCIATE CLEARLY

This is far more difficult for some than for others. The region or country or language background may make this very difficult. For instance, in the South we use soft consonants and long vowels. Hence, "door" can become "doah" and "water" becomes "wata." These regional expressions may be very comforting to one from the region and even entertaining to those from outside the region, but should be "cleaned up" enough to be easily understood.

Another trait some preachers have is to drop the last letter or even syllable of a word at the end of a sentence, making it extremely difficult to be understood. This is a great liability for one of us. Traditional church members may be able to complete the sentences or words for the preacher, but the unchurched have no idea what is missing or what is contracted.

One great way to learn to enunciate properly is to engage the skills of a singing coach, whether the preacher can sing or not. Enunciation is critical to "proper" singing technique and the vocal coach will help the preacher learn how to speak, as well as sing, more clearly.

KEY NUMBER 2—SHORTER, LESS COMPLEX SENTENCES

"Jesus was going into Jericho and a little man, a tax collector named Zaccheaus, wanted to see this famous preacher but he could not for he was too short, so he climbed up into a sycamore tree just to get to see Jesus."

That is an actual sentence from an actual sermon preached to an actual congregation. Unfortunately, it is not an unusual sentence in many sermons. How could it be improved?

"Jesus was going into Jericho. A little man, a tax collector named Zaccheaus, wanted to see him. However, he was too short to see over the crowd. So he climbed up into a sycamore tree. He wanted to see Jesus."

Shorter sentences are easier to understand and carry more punch. Long, complex sentences lose their momentum. Thoughts communicated in this way become difficult for the average listener to follow. Short and simple is almost always better than long and complex.

KEY NUMBER 3—STRONG VERBS

Too much modern preaching lacks power and punch. One primary reason is our use of the language. Strong verbs carry greater interest and paint a picture for listeners.

Look at the difference between "the father ran to his son" and "the father went to his son." The difference between two little words makes all the difference in the world in those statements. Obviously, the quote is from Luke 15 and Jesus' story of the Prodigal Son. While either statement is true, Jesus used the more vigorous verb, "ran," to communicate the power of the image he shared.

"Deny," "take up," "lay down," "lose" are the kinds of words Jesus used in communicating His gospel. These action verbs are powerful and have an impact. After all, in many ways the gospel call is a call to action, not passivity. The language used to communicate this call should be consistent with the nature of the call. Passivity and Christian discipleship do not blend very well.

KEY NUMBER 4—VOLUME

Warren began preaching before most churches and campmeetings had sound systems. Therefore, it was necessary not only to speak clearly, but also loudly. In that environment, one learned to speak to the back row of the room.

Now every little mission has a P.A. system of some description. However, this has not necessarily improved preaching. Ineffective public speakers who could not be heard before the advent of electronic amplification can now be heard—but it did not help. Now the volume is loud enough, but the ineffectiveness continues.

Therefore, when one speaks of volume in preaching, one is not necessarily speaking of great volume. Instead it is more the proper use of a variety of volumes. A whisper can be heard if done correctly. And it gives such a break from the loud.

Hence, the secret of effective use of volume is to vary the volume, consistent with the subject matter. Do not yell about a mother gently holding a dying child. But do not whisper about the One who rides the great white horse!

Normally, the volume of a sermon is to have a conversational tone about it. The variety of volume changes as the subject matter dictates the change.

Of course, some church cultures demand a certain style of preaching that dictates loud and louder. There are others that would be offended if the preacher spoke above a golf commentator's whisper. But effective preaching that will reach the unchurched is done with a variety of volumes commensurate with the subject being addressed.

KEY NUMBER 5—PACE

Someone rightly said, "Variety is the spice of life." And it is certainly true of preaching. Many preachers set a pace for their sermon early in the experience and never vary that pace. It is most effective in lulling the listener into a deep and satisfying sleep whether the pace is fast or slow.

However, the lack of variance in the pace of preaching does nothing but harm the power and impact of a sermon delivered to reach the soul of the listener. Some sermons sound as if they are preached to the steady ticking of a metronome.

Like volume, the pace of the sermon should match the subject matter. If the preacher is describing a race, the pace of the speech needs to reflect the excitement building as the runners round the track. If the issue is the slow, painful death of a loved one, the pace should be commensurate.

The key is to maintain a pace appropriate to the subject matter and to design the sermon with a variety of speech patterns included. Since boredom is the primary reason the unchurched give for not attending church, preachers must avoid the boredom of a consistent pace.

While driving on the interstate across the plains may be safe and uneventful, it is far more interesting to drive up the coast. Some will say, "Hey, we drove across the plains this summer and it was exciting!" No one ever hears a sermon in which the preacher never varies the pace and says, "It was so exciting."

KEY NUMBER 6—EYE CONTACT

Do you feel comfortable having a conversation with someone who refuses to look at you? Have you ever tried to listen actively to a preacher who will never look at you?

Effective communication is as much done with the eyes as with words. The effective preacher will look at the people to whom he or she is preaching.

Some may say, "That's easy in a small church. But what about a large sanctuary? How can you look at the people you can hardly see?"

Dr. Steve Wood preaches every Sunday to a room that seats 3,000 people—the largest sanctuary in United Methodism in the Southeast. Yet it is not uncommon for someone to leave the service saying, "I felt as if he was speaking just to me."

Why is that? Obviously much of it has to do with speaking to universal issues of the human predicament in the power of the Holy Spirit. But a great deal of the credit has to be given to the fact that Dr. Wood uses no pulpit and no notes and looks at the listeners. He maintains eye contact with the audience.

How does he do that in a room of such magnitude? He makes it a point to look at the people. Even if he cannot see their expressions or eyes, he appears to. He looks to every section of the room. He leans forward under the power of the sermon and that gives his eyes an intensity that makes the listener believe he is speaking directly to him or her.

KEY NUMBER 7—SMILE

Warren is old enough to remember when preaching was viewed as such a serious subject that a smile in the pulpit was always seen as inappropriate. As that attitude began to relax in the church, the preacher might tell something funny—usually a joke unrelated to the sermon—before he or she started preaching. However, once the serious work of preaching began, humor had no place.

We are glad those days are gone—at least in most congregations. People need to see more smiles than frowns in the pulpits of America. They certainly do not need to see the scowls that decorate the faces of many preachers.

They see the frowns and scowls enough in everyday living. They come to church to hear the good news. How do you deliver the good news with a frown?

Good news is communicated with more than just words. Try using a smile and see how much more receptive the listeners will be to the good news that we declare.

KEY NUMBER 8—REPEATED RESPONSE

Effective preaching will elicit a response from the hearer at many points in the sermon, not just at the end. Do not confuse this with telling the hearers a number of times what the expected response to the message should be. Repeated response occurs all along in the message helping the listener engage in the sermon by inviting responses to the sermon.

For example, in one congregation the known response to "God is good," is "all the time." That became meaningful during a time of a congregational disaster. However, other kinds of repeated response will also work. Do not be afraid to ask the hearer to turn to his or her neighbor and say, "God is love," or "Jesus Saves," or even, "Don't say 'no' to God." Another such response is the traditional Easter response, "Christ is Risen . . . . He is Risen Indeed."

A creative preacher will find a number of ways to move the hearer from passive to active listening. Inviting verbal response is only one of them. However, it is something of which more preachers should take advantage.

KEY NUMBER 9—LESS IS MORE

Ineffective short sermons are less ineffective than ineffective long sermons. Effective short sermons are more effective than effective long sermons.

That is to say, prepare well enough and focus clearly enough to say what needs to be said in a short rather than a long period of time. While we may not know how long Jesus preached, what we do know is most of his stories, most of his sermons, were brief, but effective.

Warren has often taught preaching courses in which the students are required to prepare four-minute sermons. Without an exception, they talk about how difficult that is. Focus is difficult for most of us to maintain. Yet an effective short sermon will be focused from beginning to end. Remember, your listeners are watching Good Morning America or MTV where nothing in the world takes more than 10 minutes to tell.

We are not suggesting preaching for four or 10 minutes. What we are suggesting is better preparation and clearer focus will enable the preacher to preach more shorter sermons effectively. Remember, "Short, boring is better than long, boring."

KEY NUMBER 10—START STRONG

Weak beginnings often result in weak endings. Begin strong. Hook the listener at the very beginning. If you do not "set the hook" the listener will often drift away while you build up to the point you want to make.

A strong start will fully engage the listener in the first one to two minutes of the sermon and will speak to something real in his or her world. If the sermon is on poverty, do not begin by telling about the situation with the poor in Africa. Tell about a child in your own neighborhood, even your own church. Make it powerful and strong—in the beginning.

If you do that you will have the opportunity of telling about the plight of children in Africa or Brazil. But first hook the listeners where they live. Begin with the known and move to the unknown.

KEY NUMBER 11—END STRONG

Often the pet dog will decide it's time to lie down. But being unable to accomplish that act, he will circle and circle, around and around, and then unceremoniously collapse in a heap on the floor. Every time he does that it reminds us of far too many sermons we have preached and heard.

Often the preacher will start circling, round and round, only to fail to find the proper place to land. Again and again the preacher will appear to be about to stop, only to go around again. Then, to top it off, when the sermon is over the end comes as a big flop.

Preacher, engage me at the beginning and at the end. I may drift off in the middle, but at least hook me and invite me to respond. Think clearly and precisely how you will end . . . then end!

KEY NUMBER 12—INVITE A RESPONSE

Inviting a response is the responsibility of the preacher. Even with all the planning and techniques outlined in this book, the preacher is still the key to eliciting a response.

Pray. Obviously a gospel preacher needs to pray for a response. "Pray the Lord of the harvest to send forth workers," is the admonishment of Jesus. Here and in many other instances Jesus encourages His followers to pray for a response to the gospel. Prayerlessness is the bane of effective preaching for a response. The preacher who allows the demands of the profession to choke out a life of faithful prayer will not see significant response to his or her preaching.

Prayer allows the work of the Holy Spirit in the heart and life of the preacher. It is the work of the Holy Spirit that reproves and convicts. It is the Holy Spirit that draws the lost to the loving Savior. An old Appalachian hymn with a haunting folk tune says:

Brethren, we have met to worship
And adore the Lord our God.
Will you pray with all your power
While we try to preach the Word?
All is vain unless the Spirit
Of the Holy One comes down.
Brethren, pray that Holy Manna
Will be showered all around.

Visualize. See in your own mind the response you believe the sermon requires. Visualize the setting, the sermon and the congregation. See the end of the sermon clearly in your mind. See what you are saying, what you are doing and what you are inviting the listeners to do. Then visualize their doing it. Actually see them responding in the way you believe God is leading you to invite a response.

Visualize how you will respond to their response. Walk through it all in your mind. If this process is bathed in prayer, you will be surprised how often what you visualized becomes reality.

Expect. God's people are an expectant people. Expectancy is woven into the fabric of the gospel. Therefore, gospel preachers need to learn to preach expectantly.

Congregations will often live up to or down to the preacher's expectations. Low expectations result in low results. Expect people to be transformed by the power of the gospel. Expect homes to be healed by the power of the gospel. Expect people to become loving, generous, faithful and spiritually maturing through the work of the Holy Spirit even in your preaching.

Prepare. No amount of praying, visualizing or expecting can overcome the failure to prepare. If the preacher will prepare for the response with all the diligence you showed in preparing for your own wedding, then you will be amazed at what God can do.

May God bless your preaching with a great harvest of transformed lives!

APPENDIX

SIX SAMPLE SERMONS

"THE COURTSHIP AWAITS, JOHN 3:16—DAN W. DUNN

> . . . God so loved the world, that he gave his only Son, that whoever believes in him should not perish but have eternal life.

A widowed grandfather was visiting his two granddaughters and woke up one morning to the smell of biscuits and bacon. Their mother told them to run upstairs and tell Grandpa breakfast was ready.

Both girls ran upstairs, but the nine-year-old outran her five-year-old sister and reached Grandpa first. She jumped onto the bed next to her grandfather, put her arms around his neck, kissed him, and whispered, "Grandpa, breakfast is ready." Finally, her little sister arrived, huffing and puffing, and as she surveyed the situation, she was very disappointed.

The big sister teased her by saying, "I've got all there is of Grandpa." Wisely, though, Grandpa smiled at the younger sister, held out his free arm, and gathered her up in his arms and hugged her.

She looked over at her big sister and said, "You may have all there is of Grandpa. But Grandpa's got all there is of me."

This morning, Dear Friends, I've got tremendous news for you. News so marvelous, so stupendous, so unbelievable, that not even Brian Williams, Katie Couric, Brit Hume and Cooper Anderson all put together can adequately cover the story or explain the implications. Unfortunately this news is so simple that we sometimes miss its importance. What is this good news? Just as that girl's grandfather had all there was of her, so too does God have all there is of you.

I hope this morning that you realize you are a unique and special creation of God. There never has been, and never will be, another you. Should the world exist for another 20 billion years, and 472 gazillion people be born during that time, there will still never be another person exactly like you.

When you stop to think about it, it's incomprehensible. After all, the basic "stuff" of which we are formed is pretty simple. For the most part, we all have two eyes, two ears, one nose, one mouth, and one head of hair. And yet from these very simple components, God has created us in such a way that we can have unlimited variations of shape, size, color, and character.

Take a minute and compare your fingerprints with the person sitting next to you. (You might want to check the condition of your nails before you do this.) Isn't it amazing that the uniqueness of your fingerprints is so scientifically certain that you could actually be convicted of murder and sentenced to death because of your fingerprints?

Now look at the ears around you. Hold on a minute, before you do, there's one ground rule: You can't laugh at each other. You can laugh *with* each other, but not at one another. Go ahead, look around and notice the ears. Notice where they're positioned. How far are they up from the shoulder? How far are they from the eyes? Put your finger in your ear and hold it out like this, now imagine a line horizontal with your eyes, and compare the differences in these distances with the people seated around you. We haven't even talked yet about the size or shape of the lobes themselves.

I was going to have us look at each other's hair, but I'm afraid that in so doing we may or may not be comparing the color of hair that God gave us (humor). Of course this is still an indication of the nuances of who we are because what we do with our hair is one of the ways we express who we are on the inside.

And so far we've talked only about the different ways people can look in their physical appearance. There is also a huge spectrum on which we fail in terms of how we think and feel and perceive the world around us. Even if we looked exactly the same on the outside, we would still be different on the inside.

I can especially identify with this, because I have a twin brother. While Don and I look a lot alike, and do in some ways think alike, we also think very differently in other ways. (In fact, he's wrong about a lot of stuff.)

We're all different. We think differently, we feel differently, we love differently, we hate differently, we process information differently, we perceive the world around us differently. We are unique.

And the really important thing about this truth is that we're not simply affirming that we are all different like the leaves of a tree are different or two snowflakes are different. I'm not speaking here about the uniqueness of nature. No, I'm talking about the uniqueness of you. *You* are unique, special, precious to God.

It would be impossible for me to overemphasize how critical it is for you to understand this truth. More than our fingerprints, our ear lobes, our hair color, our feelings, our thought processes, our sense of humor, our personality, more than all of these combined, what makes us truly unique is that God made us, God loves us, and because God loves us, what God desires is to be in a relationship with you—a living, loving, growing, life-sharing, fun-loving relationship.

> FOCUS: *What will I say?*
>
> **The focus of this sermon is prevenient grace, particularly as it is essential to the Wesleyan way of salvation. It is expressed more specifically later in the sermon as, "God wants so much to be in a relationship with you that He extends His grace to you personally, and has been extending it all along."**

As we begin our revival time together this morning it will be my privilege to share with you one of the most important concepts you will ever discover in your life: prevenient grace. "Prevenient" is spelled p-r-e-v-e-n-i-e-n-t. Prevenient grace.

Some of you may know that this is one of John Wesley's most important contributions to our theological heritage. For others of you this may not be a phrase you've heard before, or for still others you may have heard it but never really understood it.

Prevenient grace is a theological term that we use to remind ourselves that the relationship with God for which God has created us is vitally important to him. God has been working your entire life to woo you, draw you, invite you, into this relationship.

In a sense it's a little bit like the process of courtship that some of us go through. Courtship is not normally something that happens all at once. A period of time passes when a couple treads slowly and carefully, getting to know one another and learning about each other's idiosyncrasies.

Week before last a friend of mine sent me a list of responses that nine-year-old children gave to questions they were asked about love. When asked specifically to name a surefire way to make a person fall in love with you,

Alonzo said, "Don't do things like have smelly green sneakers. You might get attention, but attention ain't the same thing as love."

Camille said "Shake your hips and hope for the best."

And my favorite one was from nine-year-old Michelle, who, when asked what are most people thinking when they say, "I Love You," replied "The person is thinking: Yeah, I really do love him. But I hope he showers at least once a day."

Love is an interesting phenomenon, and relationships take time to develop. This is how it's been with me and my lovely best friend, Nancy. We've had a wonderful 30+ years together, but it didn't happen automatically. It took time for us to get to know one another, to share with each other our dreams and fears and hopes and our experiences with Christ; and because I can be so unloveable sometimes there have been times in my life when I've wondered if her love for me will last forever.

But prevenient grace means that I don't have to wonder about God. God will always love me, and will always be present in my life to invite me into a relationship with him.

And one of the things I find so refreshing about the way God courts us is that we don't have to worry about whether or not we should make the first phone call. I was so scared when I first asked Nancy out for a date, I knew I wouldn't be able to handle it if she said no. Talk about anxiety!

Of course, you have to understand a little bit about my background to grasp just how great that anxiety was. My nickname growing up was Fat Boy, and I was, so I didn't have many dates in high school. I was the guy that girls used to consider like a "brother" whom they could come to talk with about the problems they were having with their boyfriends. Talk about injustice!

Anyway, my first real date was with a girl named Esther who lived way out in the country. I didn't have my driver's license yet, so I arranged for Ricky Sauls, because he had a car, and me to double date with Esther and a friend of hers. Ricky and I drove out to Esther's house, which took about 40 minutes due to its distance, and when we arrived we discovered that Esther's friend was sick and couldn't make it.

So for my first ever real date, Ricky and I took Esther to the putt-putt on Beach Boulevard, which was at least an hour away. We had as grand a time as you can give a girl at a putt-putt course, and then we headed home.

Well, I've always been an early riser, but that also means I've also always gone to bed early, even as a teenager, so on the way back out to Esther's house I fell asleep and didn't wake up until we got there and Ricky turned off the engine. As you can imagine, Esther was not pleased, and that was the end of that relationship.

Sad to say, but that was actually the peak of my high school dating career! So you can imagine how nervous I was when I decided to ask Nancy out. I decided to take the bull by the horns and be bolder than I've ever been in my life.

She was sitting in a metal folding chair talking with friends prior to a Friday night Bible study at our church, and I walked up from behind her, leaned around, kissed her right on the mouth and said, "When we goin' out, baby?" and she said, "When you gonna ask me?" and the rest is history.

I figured that because she is so sweet and kindhearted, she wouldn't say no to an invitation like that in front of all our friends, and that helped take a little bit of the anxiety away about asking her out for that first date.

But that kind of anxiety doesn't need to be a part of our relationship with God because God always takes the initiative and pursues us throughout our lives. In fact God calls us even before we are born. As Isaiah writes in 49:1, "Listen to me . . . Before I was born the Lord called me; from my birth he made mention of my name" (NIV).

And of course it doesn't stop there. One of the most well-known passages in the entire Bible is Psalm 23. Do you remember that great line near the end, "Surely goodness and mercy shall follow me all the days of my life?"

I hope you're beginning to understand part of what the word grace really means, but for those of you English teachers and grammarians in our midst, let's take a crack at a more precise definition.

Grace = unmerited favor.

Grace is the unmerited favor of God. We do nothing to earn it, and we do not deserve it. It is experienced fully in Christ, and it is given freely as a gift.

Now, in case there are some acronym lovers in the room, I want to tell you my favorite acronym for the word grace: God's Riches at Christ's Expense.

Now that we've defined *grace*, what do we mean by the phrase, prevenient grace? *Prevenient*, as you may have already guessed, comes from the same root as the word prevent. You prevent a child from running out into the road by going in front of the child or holding the child's hand.

You protect a child from being burned in the kitchen by turning your pot handles toward the inside of the stove, and you help keep a child from being electrocuted by putting electric outlet guards around your house when your children are small. In other words, a parent is constantly doing something ahead of time on the child's behalf.

The same is true of God. Without your even being aware of it, God has been moving and working in your life.

Those of you who have dogs may own one of those leashes that retract and have a push button control you use to lock and unlock the leash as it's needed. Prevenient grace simply means that God's leash is infinite in its length.

This is not so God can keep us under His tyrannical control, but so God can keep us from running out into traffic and getting into trouble. God wants to protect us, and bring us home, into a relationship with himself. In this sense, then, prevenient grace keeps us always within God's reach.

> FORM: *How will I say it?*
>
> **The primary form of this message is the use of repetition and explanation of the theological truth of prevenient grace.**

If some of you are wondering why I'm explaining the concept of prevenient grace in so many different ways, with explanations, definitions and acronyms, well it's because I've learned through the years that communication is a very difficult art, and one has to be careful and thorough to make sure he is understood.

A wonderful illustration of the difficult intricacies of communication was once reported in Dear Abby. In a local newspaper the following classified ads appeared:

> (**Mon.**) FOR SALE - R. D. Jones has one sewing machine for sale. Phone 948-0707 after 7:00 p.m. and ask for Mrs. Kelly who lives with him cheap.
>
> (**Tues.**) NOTICE - We regret having erred in R. D. Jones' ad yesterday. It should have read: One sewing machine for sale. Cheap. Phone 948-0707 and ask for Mrs. Kelly who lives with him after 7:00 p.m.
>
> (**Wed.**) NOTICE - R. D. Jones has informed us that he has received several annoying telephone calls because of the error we made in his classified ad yesterday. His ad stands correct as follows: FOR SALE - R. D. Jones has one sewing machine for sale. Cheap. Phone 948-0707 after 7 p.m. and ask for Mrs. Kelly who loves with him.
>
> (**Thurs.**) NOTICE - I, R. D. Jones, have NO sewing machine for sale. I SMASHED IT. Don't call 948-0707, as the phone has been disconnected. I have NOT been carrying on with Mrs. Kelly. Until yesterday she was my housekeeper, but she quit.

One of my favorite parables is the parable of the lost sheep. There were 100 sheep in the fold, and 99 of them had made their way safely in. Those are really pretty good percentages, but the Good Shepherd is not satisfied with pretty good.

Like any good shepherd, he knew that sheep by name, and he was not going to rest until he found his sheep. This shepherd practiced unconditional love. According to the parable, the sheep was not stolen, it simply wasn't paying attention and got lost.

Does the shepherd, therefore, say, "It's her own fault she got lost, let her suffer the consequences, she's just getting what she deserves"? No. It doesn't matter how or why the sheep is not safe in the fold, it matters only that if you are missing, God wants you home safely.

So how do we experience God's prevenient grace? In ways too

numerous to count. If we had time today, I could ask you to share with us those occasions in your life when you knew that you knew that you knew God had gone ahead of you in a situation or circumstance to prepare the way.

You may not have realized it until after the fact, but in hindsight you saw that God's amazing grace had indeed gone before, that God had all there was of you, and had wrapped you in his loving arms.

One may experience this grace through parents, relatives, friends, events. God also seeks to influence us through the body of believers (the church), through the church's preaching, praying, loving, and teaching.

We simply don't have time to name the many ways in which God has exercised prevenient grace. But neither do we need to. In fact it might be a little dangerous because the focus of this concept is not on how God extends grace (we have a lifetime to learn and experience that), but rather on the fact that he does give grace.

So what's the point? The point is that this grace is not a nebulous, "way out there" concept just floating in the air. Yeah, yeah, God extends grace; maybe I can catch some of it sometime. *No. God wants so much to be in a relationship with you that he extends his grace to you personally, and has been extending it all along.*

Revival does not begin, as some Christians mistakenly think, with an understanding of the sinful nature of humanity. We must understand that we are sinners, to be sure, but that's not where revival begins. Revival will begin in your life when you become more aware, not of your nature, but of God's nature.

God's nature is love. He invites you to be in a loving relationship with him in all its fullness.

FUNCTION: *What is God inviting us to do?*

The function of this sermon is to invite the worshiper to respond as a courted lover to the remarkable expressions of love by the Creator God.

If you're coming to worship or attending Bible study or participating in a mission project or working in an outreach ministry or taking part in the practice of any other Christian discipline for any reason other than to nurture a relationship with God, then you have completely missed the point.

Christianity is not a religion. It is a relationship. Have you been to the Grand Canyon? Have you seen a lunar eclipse? Have you seen a sunrise or a sunset at the beach? Have you enjoyed the beauty of a rose freshly cut from your own rose bushes? The same God who is awesome enough to have created these natural wonders, that same God, wants to be in a relationship with you.

God has already called and asked you out for the first date. That's what the cross of Calvary is all about. Have you said yes? If so, will you keep the courtship going? If not, will you say yes today?

Since before you were born, and for your entire life until this very moment, God has loved you and does love you, and wants to be in a relationship with you, and unlike nine year-old Michelle's boyfriend, you don't even have to shower every day.

God invites you to come just as you are.

Our Scripture lesson today comes from John 3:16. Please recite it with me.

". . . God so loved the world that he gave His only begotten Son, that whosoever believeth in Him should not perish, but have everlasting life."

"HOLY HUG" HEBREWS 7:23-28—DAN W. DUNN

It's three o'clock in the morning. Your beautiful, loving, caring, sweet, understanding, and seven-months pregnant wife wakes you up from a deep sleep and emphatically proclaims, "I'm starving, and there's nothing left in the refrigerator; let's go somewhere and get something to eat."

Being the very loving and wise husband that you are, you immediately and even cheerfully rise from bed, throw on a pair of blue jeans and a T-shirt, help her get into the car, and take off for the nearest place to get something to eat.

Now I've got a question for you. Will you go to McDonald's? Will you go to Burger King? Will you go to Ruby Tuesdays? Will you go to Ippolito's? Will you go to East Side Mario Brothers? Grady's? Chili's? Serenades? Houlihan's? Lone Star? Outback? Coach and Six? Steak n Shake? Cookers? Sunrise Café? Subway?

There are so many restaurant choices in Atlanta, it's unbelievable. If you can think of it, there's probably a restaurant somewhere in Atlanta that serves it. But not at three o'clock in the morning. No, your choices become severely limited at that time.

Now I'm very seldom awake at three o'clock. On those rare occasions when I have been awake I don't recall looking for a place to eat, so my knowledge in this particular area of expertise is somewhat lacking. But I do know of at least one restaurant that's open 24 hours a day, 7 days a week, 365 days a year. Waffle House.

I've always wondered, why there are locks on the doors at the Waffle House? They're always open, so why bother putting locks on the doors? Perhaps it's simply the way doors come, and it would actually cost more money to order doors without locks than to order doors with locks.

Or maybe it's a safety precaution, so they can lock the doors in case they see a person in the parking lot wielding a pistol or bearing a shotgun. The locks will give them some modest protection while they call the police.

Be that as it may, the important truth in this illustration is that for that starving seven-month pregnant woman and her loving husband, there is a place they can go and get her something to eat. Someone is available to meet her need at the time she voices that need.

That's a rare thing. Even in today's world of computers and modems and web sites, fax machines, pagers and cell phones, the more common experience in life is that while we are usually fortunate to have our needs met, they often are not met in what seems to us to be a timely fashion.

At lunchtime you may choose from hundreds of restaurants and have virtually any desire related to food fulfilled. But you still have to contend with traffic to get there, wait to be seated, wait for your server to take your drink order, take your food order, and finally return in 15 minutes or longer with your lunch.

The restaurant industry is not the only place we discover 24-hour-a-day service. Dial 911 anytime day or night for police or fire emergencies. Visit most hospitals 24 hours a day (you may not receive quick service, but their emergency rooms are open). Many towing services are also on call should you have problems with your automobile.

I did get a chuckle out of one tow truck I saw several months ago. On the side of the truck was painted the company's name, and instead of the usual 24 hour service logo, they had painted on the side of the truck, 23 and 1/2 hour service available. I assume they did that just to attract attention, because they did not tell you which 30-minute segment they would be unavailable.

Turn in your Bible with me please to Hebrews 7:27.

> Now there have been many of those priests, since death prevented them from continuing in office; but because Jesus lives forever, he has a permanent priesthood. Therefore he is able to save completely those who come to God through him, because he always lives to intercede for them.
>
> Such a high priest meets our need—one who is holy, blameless, pure, set apart from sinners, exalted above the heavens. Unlike the other high priests, he does not need to offer sacrifices day after day, first for his own sins, and then for the sins of the people. He sacrificed for their sins once for all when he offered himself. For the law appoints as high priests men who are weak; but the oath, which came after the law, appointed the Son, who has been made perfect forever.

Dear friends, I have incredibly good news for you today. I have news that should make your toes tap and your hands clap and your mouth want to burst into song. I have news so good you ought to call your mama from the car phone on the way home today and share it with her. Please write this down: Waffle House did not invent 24-hour-a-day service. They got that idea from Jesus. This passage from Hebrews makes that clear so we almost can't believe it.

God revealed through Jesus' sacrifice is a 24-hour-a-day, 7-day-a-week, 365-day-a-year God. No timeouts, never "temporarily out of service," God is present for us and with us every moment of every day of our lives. As our high priest, Jesus is constantly on call, and as one of the songs in the *Cotton Patch Gospels* says, "There ain't no busy signals on the hot line to God."

Now some of you may already be familiar with the book of Hebrews, but for those of you who haven't had that pleasure yet, let me tell that these particular verses from the seventh chapter are consistent with the overall thrust of the whole letter. Hebrews was essentially written to remind early Christians that they serve a God who is forever faithful. They serve a God who never lets them down. They serve a God who never falters in love.

Hebrews is reminding us of the profound difference that exists between the Levitical high priests of the Old Testament and our high priest, whose name is Jesus. The only way the high priests in the Old Testament could claim to be a continuing intervening presence for the people of Israel was through the normal cycles of successive generations.

According to the Jewish historian Josephus, by the time of the fall of the Second Temple in A. D. 70, 83 generations of high priests had served since the time of Aaron, the first high priest. But Hebrews reminds us that that no longer matters because we now have a high priest who will never die, and therefore his priesthood will be eternal.

As our eternal high priest, Jesus will never face the Levitical priest's inevitable moment when he passes his duties to the next generation. Jesus' position as high priest is unique and unchanging. Seated at the right hand of God, he is fixed and he is forever. He is eternally available as the personal intercessory for all of humanity.

Therefore, as our eternally available, always-open conduit to God's mercy, Jesus makes it possible for each one of us to be in an immediate, intimate relationship with no less than the God of the cosmos. Jesus' sacrifice introduces each one of us to the arms of God's mercy, and takes us to the heart of God's love.

So what does this mean? *There is always someone in heaven who understands me, who loves me, and who is praying for me*. Let me repeat that. There is always someone in heaven who understands me, who loves me, and who is praying for me. And his name is Jesus.

> FOCUS: *What will I say?*
>
> **The focus of this sermon is clearly stated in the above sentence, "There is always someone in heaven who understands me, who loves me, and who is praying for me."**

Now, I want to ask you a question. Is parenting a 3-day a week job? 4-days a week? Parenting is 7-day a week job.

It is also a 24-hour a day job, so that during each of those 7 days you are a parent for all 24 hours during each day. You really are never not a parent.

> FORM: *How will I say it?*
>
> **The form of this sermon is the parallel between the nature of loving earthly caring parents and the never-ending love of God for His children.**

I want to ask all adults a question. Do your parents see you first as the mature adult and grown-up human being you are; or do they see you first as their child? They would see you first as their child.

They would also acknowledge that you are a mature adult, but they would always see you as their child. Why is that? Because as you now know, since you have your own children, once you become a parent, you are always a parent. You are never not a parent.

You will never stop loving your children even when they frustrate you. You will never stop working to help them grow and mature and learn and develop their own adulthood and their own understanding about God's love. You will probably never stop making sacrifices for their well-being. No matter how old you become and how grown-up they become, you will always be their mama or their daddy.

That's the way life is in the family of God, too, with one very important difference. In the family of God, your parent is no longer a weak and frail and sinful human being. His name is Jesus Christ; He has already made the ultimate sacrifice of love for you, and He remains forever at the Father's right hand; loving you and understanding you and guiding you and praying for you. Jesus is at the Father's right side, praying for you by name.

I have a mental list of names that I go down each day when I have my morning devotional time. I pray for Nancy and Chris and John and Matthew and Mama and Daddy and Dale and Don and Gail and Warren and Jane and Jared and Beth and Corey and John and Craig and Harvey and Buddy and Kathy and Eddie and Lee and the list goes on and on.

Whitney, Jesus Christ is speaking your name at the Father's side right now. He's standing in on your behalf. He's saying to the Father, please bless richly this person this day, and if in any frailty she offends your holiness, please accept the sacrifice of my own blood at Calvary in her behalf.

Paul, Jesus Christ is speaking your name at the Father's side right now. He's standing in on your behalf. He's saying to the Father, please bless your child richly this day, and if in his frailty and his humanity he offends your holiness, please accept the sacrifice of my own blood at Calvary in his behalf.

Sarah, Jesus Christ speaks your name at the Father's side right now. He's standing in on your behalf. He's saying to the Father, please bless your servant richly this day, and if in her frailty and her humanity she offends your holiness, please accept the sacrifice of my own blood on Calvary in her behalf.

John, Jesus Christ is speaking your name at the Father's side right now. He's standing in on your behalf. He's saying to the Father, please bless your son richly this day, and if in his frailty and his humanity he offends your holiness, please accept the sacrifice of my own blood on Calvary in his behalf.

At times even the most faithful among us wonder where God is. Situations and circumstances that we experience as human beings gnaw at our spirits and devastate our hope. Physical ailments attack our bodies and make us weak and sometimes even kill us prematurely.

Financial setbacks and relational betrayals and emotional scars damage us to our very core, and we're not sure we can make it. Sins we've committed in the past or sins we still struggle with today shame us and we are guilty and unworthy of God's love. Even the most faithful among us wonder, "Where is God?"

Where was God when my mother died in 1972? Where was God when my wife lost her father in 1975 and her mother in 1984? Where was God in June of 1987 when our house burned down and we lost 95% of what we owned? Where was God on May 11, 1996, when ValuJet flight 592 plunged to the earth? Where was God the night many years ago when my wife and I had an argument so angry and spiteful that we wondered if we'd really be able to stick together?

I do not have all the answers to these kinds of questions.

But I do know this. In each of those situations, Jesus Christ, the very Son of God, was at the Father's right side, and He was praying for everyone involved. He does the same for you, too.

An old man was dying of cancer. His daughter asked the local priest to come and pray with her father. When the priest arrived, he found the man lying in bed with his head propped up on two pillows and an empty chair beside his bed. The priest assumed that the old fellow had been informed of his visit. "I guess you were expecting me," he said.

"No, who are you?" "I'm the new associate at your parish," the priest replied. "When I saw the empty chair, I figured you knew I was going to show up." "Oh yeah, the chair," said the bedridden man. "Would you mind closing the door?" Puzzled, the priest shut the door.

"I've never told anyone this, not even my daughter," said the man. "But all of my life I have never known how to pray. At the Sunday Mass I used to hear the priest talk about prayer, but it always went right over my head. I abandoned any attempt at prayer," the old man continued, "until one day about four years ago my best friend said to me, 'Joe, prayer is just a simple matter of having a conversation with Jesus. Here's what I suggest. Sit down on a chair, place an empty chair in front of you, and in faith see Jesus on the chair. It's not spooky because He promised, "I'll be with you always." Then speak to Him and listen in the same way you're doing with me right now.' So, Father, I tried it and I've liked it so much that I do it a couple of hours every day. I'm careful, though. If my daughter saw me talking to an empty chair, she'd either have a nervous breakdown or send me off to the funny farm."

The priest was deeply moved by the story and encouraged the old guy to continue on the journey. Then he prayed with him, anointed him with oil, and returned to the rectory. Two nights later the daughter called to tell the priest that her daddy had died that afternoon. "Did he seem to die in peace?" he asked.

"'Yes, when I left the house around two o'clock, he called me over to his bedside, told me one of his corny jokes, and kissed me on the cheek. When I got back from the store an hour later, I found him dead. But there was something strange, Father. In fact, beyond strange, kinda weird. Apparently, just before Daddy died, he leaned over and rested his head on a chair beside the bed.'"

Do you need healing today? Do you need forgiveness today? Do you need mercy today? Do you need a reason to worship today? Do you need to get out of the wilderness today, and feel God's presence? Do you simply need a reminder of how awesome God is?

Will you rest your head in the lap of Jesus your High Priest?

> FUNCTION: *What is God inviting us to do?*
>
> **Relationally stated, it is to rest our heads in the lap of Jesus, our Great High Priest. It is to *experience* the caring parenting and loving care of the one who "ever lives above to intercede for me."**

Will you trust him with your life? Will you give your heart?

Never must we face alone any experience in life, or in death. No matter how great our fear, how intense our pain, how prolonged our wait, how profound our doubts—the promise of the gospel is that God is there for us 24 hours a day, 7 days a week, 365 days a year. You and I are embraced in a Holy Hug that will never let go.

"EMPTY JARS," II KINGS 4:1-7—DAN W. DUNN

The "reaching nature" of God's love is indeed amazing. God's love reaches all the way to earth in the form of Baby Jesus, right down to where we are in our present situation.

As we look together toward the gift of a new year, it's most appropriate that we remind ourselves about the incredible reaching nature of God's love. In this new year, God's love is a love that will continue to invite us and challenge us and bless us and change us and seek us.

God is like a shepherd who has 99 sheep safely in the fold, but still seeks the one sheep that is lost. God is like a father whose son has wasted his inheritance and brought shame to the family name, but when he comes home he is welcomed with open arms and a gigantic party to celebrate his safe return. God is a like a woman who has lost a silver coin and turns her house upside down until she finds it.

It's important for us to be reminded that God's love will indeed be reaching for us during this new year.

God's love will be reaching through our fear.
God's love will be reaching through our sickness.
God's love will be reaching through our health.
God's love will be reaching through our isolation.
God's love will be reaching through our pride.
God's love will be reaching through our heartache.
God's love will be reaching through our joy.
God's love will be reaching through our grief.
God's love will be reaching through our happiness.

Whatever our situation, whether good, bad, or indifferent, God's love is still reaching, because that's the nature of God. He will always be reaching for us, extending his love toward us, inviting us to enjoy the fullness of a personal relationship with him.

One of the things that saddens me most in my ministry is the knowledge that so many church folks live for years without ever really understanding the depth of God's love for them, and the tremendous joy and peace and grace and abundant living that God desires for them.

It seems as though many of us go through our Christian walk with blinders on. For some reason we just can't see that God's ultimate desire is for us to experience the fullness of a vibrant, transformational, life-giving relationship with God. To quote a wonderful Southern expression, "God loves the fire out of you," and he wants more than anything to shower you with "joy unspeakable and full of glory," as the Apostle Paul puts it. Isn't that what you want for the people you love?

Don't you want your mother or father or son or daughter or husband or wife—don't you want loved ones to experience life filled with joy and peace and love and grace and blessings and effectiveness and fulfillment? If we want those things for the people we love, why would we think that God would want anything less for us, whom God loves?

Think of someone right now whom you love, and bring a picture to your mind of something that you deeply desire for them to experience.

Maybe it's a son or a daughter, and you deeply desire that they would find a loving Christian spouse with whom they can share the rest of their life. God's desire for that blessing in their life is even stronger than yours.

Maybe it's a grandmother or a favorite uncle, and you deeply desire that they would be cured of their illness and restored to optimal physical health. God's desire for that blessing in their life is even stronger than yours.

Maybe it's a father or a mother, and you deeply desire that they would be healed of the pain and grief and bitterness that still lingers from their divorce. God's desire for that blessing in their life is even stronger than yours.

Maybe it's a brother or a sister, and you deeply desire that they would be cured of their addiction to alcohol and find some sense of happiness or stability. God's desire for that blessing in their life is even stronger than yours.

No one loves like God. No one blesses like God. No one cares for people like God. No one desires the absolute best for you more than God. No one loves you as God does.

That being the case, what is it that keeps you from experiencing the fullness of God's intended blessings in your life? What is it that blocks you from receiving all he has in store for you? What is it that gets in the way of your being the person God has designed you to be?

Judging from our Scripture passage this morning, one of the most important factors is that we don't understand the principle of empty jars. The principle of empty jars is simply this: when the jars get full, the oil stops flowing.

> FOCUS: *What will I say?*
>
> **This sermon will focus on the requirement of our partnering with God in creating the avenues of blessing, increasing our capacity for the blessing of God.**

The story from II Kings is one of those exquisite little gems that may be found throughout the Old Testament. The widow comes to the prophet Elisha to seek counsel about her desperate financial situation. Her husband has died and left her with a large debt, and the creditor has come to say that he plans to take her two sons away as payment.

Elisha asks her what she has in the house that might be of some value, and she remembers she has a little oil. Upon hearing this, Elisha instructs her to go and gather jars from her neighbors, then shut the doors so no one else will see what they're doing, and start pouring that little bit of oil into the jars.

Her sons gather the jars and they start pouring, and amazingly enough, her tiny bit of oil continues to flow until there are no jars left. The prophet then tells her to go and sell the oil, and not only will she have enough to pay her current debt, but there will also be enough left over for them to continue to live on.

We can learn a very important truth from this story, and that is that more often than not, the primary factor that limits God working in our lives is our capacity to receive the blessings God wants to give us. God's capacity to bless us is unlimited, but our capacity to receive those blessings is not. To use the imagery from the story, God's supply of oil is never-ending, but our supply of empty jars is not.

There are two aspects of this truth that help us understand it more fully. The first is that God loves us too much to bless us beyond that which we can receive. He wants to bless us richly; he wants us to experience the joy of a personal relationship with him, God wants us to be effective in serving others; he wants us to experience grace and mercy and peace, but God will bless us only to the point that we can handle.

God knows us better than we know ourselves, and he knows what blessings we are in a position to receive and use. God knows that if we don't have empty jars available for him to pour the oil of blessing into, then to continue pouring his oil in our lives would actually do us more harm than good.

We would be put in the same situation in which Lucy Ricardo found herself in that classic episode when she was working in a chocolate factory and the conveyor belt started coming faster than she was able to keep up with. What a mess! The same sort of mess is what our lives would look like if God poured out his blessings without our being in a position to receive them, and God loves us too much to let that happen. Those of you who are parents will understand this principle.

We learn from the principle of empty jars that: God more often than not wants us to do something to contribute to the blessings we receive. It is not always the case that God waits for us to provide an empty jar before he will pour out a blessing to us. But it is certainly true far more often than not. Put simply, God wants us to cooperate with him as he works in our lives.

FORM: *How will I say it?*

The primary literary tool will be the contrast and comparison of the old jars and new jars needed in one's life to receive God's blessing. After all, when you run out of jars . . . the oil of God's blessing stops flowing.

This is seen consistently throughout the Bible:

When God parted the Red Sea for the children of Israel in

the book of Exodus, he waited until Moses stretched out his hand over the waters, as God had commanded him to do.

When the Syrian general, Naaman, discovered he had leprosy, he visited the prophet of God and was told that God would heal him if he would wash in the Jordan River seven times.

When Jesus fed the 5,000 he used the five loaves and two fish that a little boy had brought for his lunch.

When Jesus turned the water into wine in the second chapter of John, notice that he didn't create wine from nothing. First, he asked the servants to fill the jars to the brim with water.

Even when Jesus raised Lazarus from the dead in John 11, before performing this act of resurrection, he asked them to remove the stone from the entrance to the tomb.

It is clear throughout the Bible that God wants us to be active participants in our relationship with him. Yes, God loves us and wants the best for us. Yes, God's love is a seeking, inviting, generous, amazing love. And, yes, God wants us to do our part. God wants us to place ourselves in what we might call a position of receptivity. He wants us to make available empty jars, because when the jars get full...(the congregation was invited to respond, "the oil stops flowing").

If I leave here today and somehow break my arm, neither I nor my doctor can heal that broken arm, nor are we responsible for healing it. Only God finally heals. But I am responsible for finding my way to the doctor and the doctor is responsible for placing that arm in a cast. That cast represents for my arm a position of receptivity, it makes available to God an empty jar into which he can pour the oil of blessing, because when the jars get full...("the oil stops flowing").

If I am struggling with an addiction to alcohol and I want to ask for God's help, that would be fantastic. God would love to set me free from that addiction, but he would also probably want me to ask for help from other people in my life, such as Alcoholics Anonymous or someone from a counseling center. Attending AA or counseling would put me in a position of receptivity, that would make available to God an empty jar into which he can pour the oil of blessing, because when the jars get full...("the oil stops flowing").

If I want to grow in my understanding of the Bible and how to apply its truths to my everyday life, God naturally would be thrilled to help me with that, but he would also expect me to purchase a Bible if I don't already own one, and would expect me to read it, and would probably appreciate my participating in a group or a Sunday school class. Those things would put me in a position of receptivity. They would make available to God an empty jar into which he could pour the oil of blessing, because when the jars get full...("the oil stops flowing").

I cherish for you that in the year 2002 the oil of God's blessings would flow richly and deeply, but for that to happen, you must make available empty jars, you need to increase your capacity for God to work in your life. You can do that in two basic ways.

First, pour "stuff" out of jars that you already have.

You could decide that today is the day you'll pour out that spirit of unforgiveness that has been filling up one of your jars and has been blocking the love of God.

You could decide that today is the day you'll get rid of that sludge of envy that's been filling up one of your jars and has been blocking the deep contentment of God from your life.

You could decide that today is the day you'll dispose of that moldy batch of greed that's been filling up one of your jars and has been blocking the joy of a generous spirit.

You could decide that today is the day you'll pour out that smelly supply of low self-esteem that's been filling up one of your jars and has been blocking God's desire to use you in ministry with other people.

You could decide that today is the day you'll get rid of that old supply of selfishness that's been filling up one of your jars and has been blocking the tremendous fulfillment of serving others.

You could decide that today is the day you'll start emptying some of the jars you already have so that God can do some amazingly wonderful things in your life, as God so deeply desires to do.

Second, you can create some new empty jars in your life.

You might decide that this is the week you'll begin reading your Bible on a regular basis.

You might decide that this is the week you'll offer to help with the children's ministry.

You could decide that this is the week you'll sign up for a mission trip.

You could decide that this is the week you'll start working with a nursing home ministry.

> You could decide that this is the week you'll visit a Sunday school class.
>
> You could decide that this is the week you'll contact the church about helping with student ministry.
>
> You could decide that this is the week you'll check into being part of a men's accountability group.
>
> You could decide that this is the week you'll start making available new empty jars, so God can do some amazingly wonderful things in your life, which is his deepest desire.

You see, it is true that when the jars run out . . . but the corollary is also true: Keep an empty jar available, and the oil will keep flowing.

Keep advancing your position of receptivity and God will continue to work in your life. Keep an empty jar available, and the oil will keep flowing.

> FUNCTION: *What is God inviting us to do?*
>
> **This sermon is designed to help the worshiper identify one or more things that block the flow of God's blessing as well as identify at least one new avenue of blessing open for that same grace.**

If you'll keep increasing your capacity for his grace, God will bring about amazing miracles in your life. Keep an empty jar available, and the oil will keep flowing.

If you'll empty old jars and also produce some new ones, God will transform your living in surprising ways. Keep an empty jar available, and the oil will keep flowing.

And the intriguing thing about all this is that the choice is ours to make. In this particular case, we actually have more power than

God. We aren't more powerful, but we do have more power. Since God has given us free will, he thereby has also placed a self-imposed limit on when, how, and where he will act.

God will not act for us if we choose not to have empty jars available. We are the ones who decide how many available jars we have. In that sense, we have more power than God. The choice is ours. The choice is mine. The choice is yours.

Begin or continue to live a full, abundant, effective, victorious life for and with Jesus. The choice is yours to make, and now is the time to make it—not next year, not next month, not next week, but today.

> God's love is reaching for you today.
> Do you have a jar ready?
> God's grace is reaching for you today.
> Do you have a jar ready?
> God's mercy is reaching for you today.
> Do you have a jar ready?
> God's joy is reaching for you today.
> Do you have a jar ready?
> God's calling to effective service is reaching for you today.
> Do you have a jar ready?

God loves the fire out of you, Dear Friends, and he wants to bless you beyond your imagination. This year, this month, this week, I invite you and encourage you to keep empty jars available for the oil of God's blessing. You'll be amazed at the results.

Make a list of at least two old jars in your life to empty. These may include greed or lust or cynicism or dishonesty or fear or addiction or some other thing that is filling jars so that God can not pour the oil of blessing into your life. On the other side, list at least one new jar that you will open to receive God's blessing. Perhaps it is to begin tithing. Perhaps it is to go on a mission trip. Perhaps it is to volunteer each week in a needy place. What new jar of blessing is God inviting you to open to his presence?

"BELIEVE AND CONFESS," ROMANS 10:8-17—WARREN LATHEM

> "The word is near you; it is in your mouth and in your heart," that is, the word of faith we are proclaiming: That if you confess with your mouth, "Jesus is Lord," and believe in your heart that God raised him from the dead, you will be saved. For it is with your heart that you believe and are justified, and it is with your mouth that you confess and are saved. As the Scripture says, "Anyone who trusts in him will never be put to shame." For there is no difference between Jew and Gentile—the same Lord is Lord of all and richly blesses all who call on him, for, "Everyone who calls on the name of the Lord will be saved." How, then, can they call on the one they have not believed in? And how can they believe in the one of whom they have not heard? And how can they hear without someone preaching to them? And how can they preach unless they are sent? As it is written, "How beautiful are the feet of those who bring good news!" But not all the Israelites accepted the good news. For Isaiah says, "Lord, who has believed our message?" Consequently, faith comes from hearing the message, and the message is heard through the word of Christ.

I've always been amazed by what people will believe. Recent grocery store tabloids had these headlines:

Dinosaurs Honked Like Buicks

Cow Mattresses Help Cows Produce More Milk

Mom-To-Be On Diet Of Only Chicken, Lays Huge Egg

WWII Bomber Found On The Moon

Woman Gives Birth To 2 Year Old Baby: Child Walks & Talks in 3 Days

Adam & Eve's Bones Found In Asia: Eve Was a Space Alien?

People will read and believe this nonsense, but refuse to believe in Jesus Christ. And there has never been a time in the history of this country when we needed more to believe in and trust in Jesus Christ than we do today.

Here are some data from the National Center for Health Statistics: "The rate of violent crime in the United States is worse than that of any other industrialized country. Our population has increased by 41 percent since 1960, but violent crimes have increased more than 500 percent, and total crimes more than 300 percent. Eight out of every 10 Americans will be victims of violent crime at least once in their lives. The U.S. homicide rate for 15-24 year-olds is seven times higher than Canada's and 40 times higher than Japan's. The United States is at or near the top in rates of abortion, divorce and unwed births. And in elementary and secondary education, we are at or near the bottom in achievement scores. Since 1960 we have witnessed a more than 400 percent increase in illegitimate births, a more than 200 percent increase in the teenage suicide rate, and a drop of 75 points in average SAT scores. Thirty-two million dollars was spent last year on metal detectors in American public schools."[1]

We are a nation that has lost our way. We are lost and we do not know where to turn. Yet our fear and insecurity cause us to follow almost any way that promises a way out of the hideous condition of our communities and our nation.

It reminds me of a story about University of Illinois football coach Bob Zuppke. He was renowned for the fire and fervor of his half-time pep talks. One afternoon, his team hit the locker room after the first half well behind in both points and enthusiasm. Zuppke began talking to them and the more he talked, the louder and more dramatic his voice became. The momentum built in the players. Then the coach pointed to the door at the far end of the locker room and said, "Now go out there and win this game!" Filled with emotion the players got off the bench, ran toward the door and charged through it. But it was the wrong door, and one by one they fell into the swimming pool!

It is one thing to be all charged up; it is quite another thing to be headed in the right direction.

> FOCUS: *What then shall I say?*
>
> **The focus of this sermon is to declare the absolute necessity and possibility of a saving relationship with Jesus Christ, leading the worshiper into that relationship of which Paul writes.**

We are a nation that has lost its way. But we, as individuals, have lost our own way. This is still a nation made up of its people. And if you are as disgusted as I am at the debate that sometimes rages in Congress, please be aware that it is simply a reflection of a people who have lost their way.

However, today, I am not concerned with helping a nation find its way. I am concerned with helping you. For many of you who come into this church today are lost. That's right, lost!

What do I mean by lost? Just the opposite of what it means to be saved.

A little boy was studying synonyms and antonyms. His teacher said, "What is the opposite of lost?" He answered, "Saved." The teacher said, "No, that is not right. The opposite of lost is found." The little boy responded with, "I'll tell you this: When you get saved, you've been found!"

FORM: *How will I say it?*

The form of this sermon is to take a "troublesome" word for enlightened Americans and reveal the true and essential nature of the necessity of being saved.

In a world that is so confused and lost, in a world that needs to be saved, in a world where many of us who come to church today are lost, it is important for me to tell you how you can be saved.

No word in the Christian vocabulary makes people feel more uncomfortable than the word "saved." People cringe when they hear it. Perhaps it conjures up visions of hot-eyed, zealous button-holers—usually with bad breath—who walk up and grab you and say, "Brother, are you saved?" Or perhaps it raises visions of a tiny band of Christians at a street meeting in front of a saloon singing, "Give the winds a mighty voice, Jesus saves! Jesus saves!" Whatever the reason, I do know that people become bothered by this word.

When I was in college, if a person walked up to me in the cafeteria and asked, "Is this seat saved?" I would respond by saying, "I don't know, but we're praying for it."

Somehow this word "saved" threatens all our religious complacency and angers the self-confident and the self-righteous alike. However, it is imperative that we talk about the fact that people need to be saved, you need to be saved, because we are lost.

We can never deal realistically with life until we face up to this fundamental fact: People are not waiting until they die to be lost. They are already lost. This lost condition is not that we may have lost our way in no more serious way than getting lost on an unfamiliar road in a strange city. No, this is like being lost, out of gas, broke, hungry and cold on a dark, narrow, dead-end road in North Georgia and hearing someone picking on a banjo the tune from "Deliverance."

This kind of "lost" is what the Bible refers to as being aliens and strangers, it is being dead in trespasses and sins, it is to be blind, deaf, mute, homeless, hungry, thirsty, guilty. We are lost and we need a savior.

It is the grace of God that reaches out to us and calls us out of that lost condition and gives us an opportunity to come to Christ and be saved. Therefore "saved" is a perfectly legitimate word to use. It makes us uncomfortable only when we refuse to face the fact that men and women are lost. We are born into a perishing race in which our humanity is being put to improper uses and is gradually deteriorating and falling apart, and we are facing an eternity of separation from God.

We are lost and we need a savior. Therefore, when the angels sang the song to the shepherds in the darkness of the night on the plains of Bethlehem, and the glory of the Lord broke out upon them and the angel said to them, ". . . behold, I bring you good tidings of great joy, which shall be to all people. For unto you is born this day in the city of David a Saviour, who is Christ the Lord" (Luke 2:10-11), it was God announcing a solution to our problem, a way out of our predicament. A Savior is born!

And this brings us to why today's Scripture lesson is so important. It gives us what is required of us to be saved, to benefit from the gift of the Savior. You see, it is not enough to recognize that we are in fact lost, nor is it enough to know that God provided a Savior in the person of Jesus Christ.

Paul states very clearly what is required: " . . . if you confess with your mouth, Jesus is Lord, and believe in your heart that God raised him from the dead, you will be saved."

Paul tells us here that Jesus is Lord, and if you have come to the place where you believe in your heart that He is risen and available, and you are ready to say to yourself, "Jesus is my Lord," then God acts. At that moment God does something. No one of us can do it, but God can.

God begins to bring about all that is wrapped up in this word "saved."

> Your sins are forgiven.
> God imparts to you a standing of righteous worth in his sight.
> He loves you.
> He gives you the Holy Spirit to live within you.
> He makes you a child in his family.
> He gives you an inheritance for eternity.
> You are joined to the body of Christ as members of the family of God.
> You are given Jesus Himself to live within you, to be your power over evil—over the world, the flesh, and the devil—and you will live a life entirely different than you lived before.

That is what happens when you confess with your mouth that Jesus is Lord and believe in your heart that God raised him from the dead.

But what does it mean to confess with your mouth that Jesus is Lord and believe in your heart that God raised him from the dead? Is it simply to say the words like a magical incantation? Is it simply orthodox or right thinking? What does it mean?

It is helpful to see that nowhere in all the Scriptures are we ever asked to believe in Jesus as Savior. We are asked to believe in him as Lord. When you believe in him as Lord, he becomes your Savior. But you don't accept Christ as a Savior—you accept him as Lord, as the one who is in charge of all things, including you. When you come to that point, when you respond with the whole person, then God says the work of redemption is done. The miracle occurs.

- He is Lord of our past, to forgive us our sins.
- He is Lord of our present, to dwell within us and to guide and direct and control every area of our lives.
- He is Lord of our future, to lead us into glory at last.
- He is Lord of life, Lord of death, he is Lord over all things.

"If you confess with your mouth, 'Jesus is Lord,' and believe in your heart that God raised him from the dead, you will be saved." That is the way it happens. At this time of the year I always think of that beautiful little carol, "O Little Town of Bethlehem." I love the third verse:

How silently, how silently,
The wondrous gift is given!
So God imparts to human hearts
The blessings of His heaven.
No ear may hear His coming,
But in this world of sin,
Where meek souls will receive Him still,
The dear Christ enters in.

To confess with my mouth that Jesus is Lord is to surrender my life to him. It is to give him control of my immediate and eternal destiny. It is to release the decision-making power of my life and turn it over to him. As someone has said, either Jesus is Lord of all in our lives or he is not Lord at all.

To confess and believe involves all of who you are: your present, your past and your future. It engages your desires, your will, your longings. It captivates your dreams, your devotion, your allegiance.

If it is all about the Lordship of Christ and our commitment to Him, then why all this fuss about Christmas and the birth of a Baby who will save His people from their sins? Why all this talk about a Savior? Why all this story of the miracle of grace?

It is to bring us to a place where we can confess with our mouths that Jesus is Lord and believe in our hearts that God has raised him from the dead so we can be saved. And the miracle of Christmas, the miracle of the Incarnation, the story of a Savior is the work of grace, prevenient grace, given to us to bring us to faith in and commitment to Christ.

FUNCTION: ***What is God inviting us to do?***

The function of this sermon is to awaken the hunger for God and the need for a Savior and invite the worshiper to confess publicly the lordship of Christ.

> A child who suffers from severe malnutrition, mercifully loses all appetite. After weeks of nothing to eat, the desire for food finally shuts down. When aid workers begin to dip a sugar-sweetened finger in such a child's mouth, tears are the first sign of hope. The cries of hunger mark the return of the child's appetite and the birth of hope.
>
> The gospel of God's grace awakens our hunger. The Holy Spirit births in us the sweet reassurance that in Christ we are God's beloved sons and daughters in whom God is pleased. We cry in pain over our malnutrition and seek true food.[2]

So many of us have been spiritually starving for so long that our appetite for spiritual nourishment has shut down. But then comes the story of Christmas, the birth of a Savior, the miracle of the Incarnation, and by God's grace, our hunger is awakened. We begin to cry again, cry over our spiritual malnutrition.

Today, are you hungry? As we hear again the songs of Christmas, the words of the angels, as we visit again the scene in Bethlehem, are you beginning to sense just how malnourished your soul really is? Are you sensing something of the magnitude of your horrible lost condition? Are you aware of your need of a Savior?

Then praise God! For now you can "Confess with your mouth that Jesus is Lord and believe in your heart that God has raised him from the dead, and you will be saved!"

Hear that? You will be saved! You will be saved!

[1] John Rodden of the University of Texas in "Dimensions of Forgiveness," Vital Speeches, LXIII [September 15, 1997], 712.

[2] Tim Dearborn, Taste & See: Awakening Our Spiritual Senses (Downers Grove: Ill.: Intervarsity Press, 1996), 53.

"JESUS LOVED UNCONDITIONALLY," MATTHEW 9:35-38—WARREN LATHEM

> Jesus went through all the towns and villages, teaching in their synagogues, preaching the good news of the kingdom and healing every disease and sickness. When he saw the crowds, he had compassion on them, because they were harassed and helpless, like sheep without a shepherd. Then he said to his disciples, "The harvest is plentiful but the workers are few. Ask the Lord of the harvest, therefore, to send out workers into his harvest field."

"When he saw the crowds, he had compassion on them . . . ."

> FOCUS: *What will I say?*
> **The focus of this sermon is the invitation of Jesus to pray for laborers in the harvest fields.**

Jesus had just gone through all the towns and villages of Galilee. It was a heavily populated area. Its nickname was "Galilee of the nations." Many people were there, several different kinds of people. As Jesus moved among the great crowds, He was moved by what He saw.

Dr. Hunt, former senior minister of Mount Pisgah United Methodist Church, was a business consultant with one of the large national consulting firms before answering God's call to preach the gospel. He was in New York on business. He had to step over yet another homeless man trying to stay warm over a steam vent in the sidewalk. God used that experience to stop Allen in his tracks and turn him in a new direction. It was from that moment he began to see people differently than he had ever seen them. He became the senior minister of a church of 7,000 members because he, like Jesus, saw, really saw the crowds.

One member of our church has helped to build several churches around the world. She recently returned from a trip to Russia where she visited the church built in the first Methodist church building in Russia—a building she and some others from Mount Pisgah provided. She helped build the church because she knew people needed the gospel. However, on her visit, she saw the crowds of children, orphans, who need everything, not only a church. She's about gone crazy trying to help those parentless children. She's even almost talked her sister into adopting one.

Another member of our church "saw" the multitudes in prison in America and is developing a ministry to them, a ministry you can be involved with.

I realized in 1996 that there was no United Methodist church in Venezuela. He has helped us sponsor the fledgling conference there, where now over 25 churches have already been formed and new ones are being planted on a regular basis.

A number of years ago, not too long after the Kroger store was built at Haynes Bridge and Old Alabama in Alpharetta, Georgia, my wife and I had stopped in to pick up bread or milk or something. Like the wonderful husband I am, I dropped her off right at the door and pulled out into the lot to wait. As I sat there, I began to "see" the crowds. I was moved to tears because I realized so many of them were lost and without Christ, so many of them were "harassed and helpless," so many of them "were like sheep without a shepherd." I had been to Kroger many times and had seen the same things, but I had never really seen them with my heart, just my eyes.

That experience fueled much of our church's commitment to make disciples. That experience is part of the reason we are among the top four or five churches in the denomination every year in the number of new converts and among the top three or four in worship attendance in the denomination. That experience helped shape why we have this sanctuary, why we have purchased more than 40 acres, why we have a school with more than 1,000 kids, why we will build a larger sanctuary, why we have a Women's Crisis Pregnancy Center, why we have a Counseling Center, why we have a Christian Recreation ministry, why we serve over 1,000 kids each year in VBS, why we will adopt so many kids through Angel Tree, and the list goes on and on. These things and others have been done for many reasons, not the least of which is the experience I had in the Kroger parking lot that day when I "saw" the crowds.

Unfortunately, many Christians are content to be "Christian" for themselves, to hug the gospel to themselves, to sit in their own little church, to feed upon the Word on their own, to forget about a world that is lost and dying without Christ.

You know it is so. That is why fewer than half of you even make a pledge to give money to support the mission of the church. You are selfish and self-absorbed. You don't care about the crowds who are harassed and helpless, like sheep without a shepherd. All you care about is yourself.

You want only to feel good. You come to church to feel better. You want a good service. You want to be entertained. You want us to lift you up. You want to be fed. You say, "I have got to go somewhere so I can be fed." So you come here.

It's time you started feeding some other folks. Its time you quit being so consumed with your own selfish needs and started making a difference in the crowds who are "harassed and helpless."

When Jesus saw the crowds, Jesus saw people.

FORM: *How will I say it?*

The method used in this sermon is observation, confrontation and invitation. It is reminiscent of Nathan's exposing David, "You are the man"! It goes further by inviting the worshiper to become a part of the solution to the observation of the shepherdless multitudes.

Do you see the people on their drive to work or do you see only a traffic jam? Do you see the people at a Braves game or do you see nothing but a crowd of nameless folks who mean nothing to you? When you are walking into the theater do you see the people? Do you see them?

To see the crowds is a moving experience. Why? Most are lost and without Christ. Most are perishing. Most are in danger of the hell Jesus spoke so often.

Most of the people on the highway do not know Jesus. Does it matter? It mattered enough for Jesus to die for them. Most of the folks at the Braves game do not know Christ. Does it matter? It mattered to Jesus. Most of the people you watch that movie with do not know Christ. Does it matter?

See the crowds in church—more than 3,000 weekly and more than 6,000 on Christmas Eve. Do you see that many of these folks do not know Jesus? Do you care? Are you moved with compassion?

> Jesus saw the crowds. All kinds of people:
> Good people and bad people;
> Faithful people and unfaithful people;
> Honest people and dishonest people;
> Honorable people and dishonorable people;
> Reputable people and disreputable people;
> Religious people and irreligious people;
> Healthy people and sick people;
> Rich people and poor people.

"When he saw the crowds he had compassion on them."

Jesus' response to all these different folks was one of compassion, care, concern, empathy, love that makes a difference. Why compassion?

"They were harassed and helpless, like sheep without a shepherd." They were lost, wandering, pursuing, searching for something to satisfy, something to comfort, something to give direction to their lives.

Do you care? Do you have compassion? Do you love enough to make a difference? Jesus did. All year we have been asking the question: "What did Jesus do?" Today we see that Jesus loved unconditionally.

He didn't pre-qualify the recipients of his love. He didn't segregate those he would have compassion for from the ones who would get no compassion. He didn't discriminate. He had compassion on the crowds, saints and sinners, rich and poor, people like him and people unlike him.

He cared. Jesus cared, Jesus had compassion because they were like sheep without a shepherd. In the New Testament, shepherd is a word often associated with pastor. In fact, I learned in teaching in the seminary in Mexico City that there really is no Spanish word for "shepherd" other than "pastor." Pastor means "shepherd." Shepherd means "pastor." Jesus is the *Great* Shepherd of our souls, the *Great* Pastor.

Jesus was concerned for the crowds; He had compassion on the crowds because they had no pastor, no shepherd, no one to care for their souls.

You have a pastor, in fact, several. However, most folks have no pastor. Often the pastors of this church are called to do a funeral for someone who simply didn't know a single minister on which to call for the funeral. Folks who didn't have a pastor and no one in the family who has a pastor. So we go into a chapel to do a funeral for someone we do not know, for people we have never met.

You may think that is a rare experience. Wrong! There are 250,000 people who live within five miles of this church. Even with multiple services at this time we have far fewer than 25,000 seats in churches in this community. Only one in ten even attend church, and fewer than that on any given Sunday.

People need a pastor. People need someone to care for their souls. People need someone who will lead them to Christ. People need someone who will help them grow in the faith. People need someone who will equip them for ministry in the world. People need a shepherd, people need a pastor.

One of the things we want to do in the new millennium at Mount Pisgah is recruit and train pastors to plant churches in North Fulton, Venezuela, Cherokee County, Henry County, Orlando, Lexington, Raleigh, New York and Russia and whereever God sends people to serve. We will recruit and train lay missionaries. We will recruit and train men and women who will give their lives to reach a lost and dying world.

We already have the commitment of a seminary to help us in the training of these shepherds. We will design our own training program for those who have no desire for ordination. We will partner together to train these men and women who share the compassion, the unconditional love of Jesus for a lost and dying world.

THE HARVEST IS PLENTIFUL BUT THE WORKERS ARE FEW.

There are lots of preachers. There's one in the news about every night for committing a crime. However, there are few "workers" in the harvest.

For example, did you know that 40-50% of all 30,000 United Methodist churches in America do not win one person to Christ in a year? Did you know that almost half of the 300,000 Protestant churches in America do not win one person to Christ in any given year?

The workers are few. Every year the North Georgia Conference of the UMC has more people wanting to serve churches than we have churches to serve. Yet every year there is a dearth of spiritual leadership from people who will work in the harvest. Every year the bishop has far fewer workers than he has places to work. Oh, there are plenty of bodies, few workers. We need some missionary pastors:

People who will go to work in the harvest;
People who understand the condition of the human soul;

People who know the human predicament;
People who know Christ and his power to save;
People who have a passion to win the lost;
People who care for the whole world;
People who will become Biblically literate;
People who will give themselves to a life of service;
People who seek no worldly gain;
People who are unencumbered with the cares of this world;
People who will lay aside everything for Jesus' sake;
People who are called to make a difference in the world.

We will train and send out missionaries/preachers/pastors/ shepherds who understand the charge of John Wesley to his preachers, "You have nothing to do but save souls."

This is a call to prayer. "Ask the Lord of the harvest, therefore, to send out workers into his harvest field."

The fields are ripe and ready for harvest. People are hungry for spiritual nourishment. People are thirsty for meaning for life. People are dying without hope. People are living without hope. People want someone to show them the way. People want an authentic witness for Christ. The people are ready. The fields are ripe. The harvest is plentiful.

FUNCTION: *What is God inviting us to do?*

The function of this sermon is to create a community that will faithfully pray for laborers in the Lord's harvest fields and thereby possibly hear and respond to God's call upon their own lives while praying this prayer.

Pray for workers. Why?
Because you share the awareness of Jesus for the crowds—you see.
Because you share the compassion of Jesus—you care.

Because you share the burden of Jesus—you act.
Pray for workers. ***WARNING!*** Be careful what you pray for.

You may be the answer to your prayer. Your child may be the answer to your prayer. Your spouse may be the answer to your prayer. Your parent may be the answer to your prayer.

However, pray. Pray because you know Jesus and you care about eternal lives and destinies of the great crowds who do not know Him! Pray for workers.

Will you pray for workers? If you will make workers in the kingdom a matter of daily prayer, would you simply raise your hand? Now you are committing to pray for God to send forth workers into the harvest field of the kingdom. And you are committing to pray every day. Let us pray together as the body of Christ for God to send forth workers.

Since this sermon was preached, remarkable things have happened. The people prayed for laborers in the Lord's harvest field. Several members of this congregation have answered the call to ministry and some to the mission field. The church has planted new congregations in Russia, Venezuela, North Georgia, Africa, New York, and Costa Rica. A new theological seminary was founded in Venezuela, The Wesley Seminary of Venezuela, where over 80 students and pastors are receiving an undergraduate-level education and practical theological training. The Wesley Association of Venezuela has been incorporated as has Venezuela for Christ, Inc., a Georgia nonprofit corporation to advance the work of the UMC in Venezuela (www.venezuelaforchrist.blogsport.com). A unique program called Lay Missionary Training was born and has become a training program of the North Georgia Conference Board of Laity. More than 100 people have been trained to do ministry *outside* the local church to reach the lost of their community and world. Outstanding ministries have been birthed by these participants including a ministry with the homeless, an equestrian ministry with troubled girls, a ministry with AIDS orphans in Kenya, a ministry with stroke victims, a ministry of a local food-and-clothing bank, a ministry with abused women, a ministry of short-term mission teams, a ministry with immigrant populations, English as a Second Language ministries, and many others. Additionally, several have heard the call to ordained ministry and are serving churches or attending seminary or both. For more information visit the North Georgia web site (www.ngumc.org) and click on Board of Laity. Also, a consulting firm was created to work with local churches to facilitate their effectiveness in reaching the unchurched with the gospel of Christ. This consulting group has worked with small churches as well as some of the largest churches in the denomination. For more information visit www.aslangroup.com. All of these ministries have been initiated by Dr. Warren Lathem and supported by scores of faithful servants of Christ. Pray for laborers in the Lord's harvest fields!

"DOES GOD CARE?" LUKE 12:6-7—WARREN LATHEM

"Are not five sparrows sold for two pennies? Yet not one of them is forgotten by God. Indeed, the very hairs of your head are all numbered. Don't be afraid; you are worth more than many sparrows."

> FOCUS: *What will I say?*
>
> **This sermon attempts to give context to the words, "God cares."**

Kirk was having one of those bad days where everything seems to go wrong. One thing after another until, at the close of the day, he lay in bed absolutely exhausted. As he thought over the day, he became more and more upset until he finally blurted out, "Why me, God? Why does everything always go wrong for me?" Suddenly, the ceiling of his room was pulled back, and a huge hand with an outstretched finger came down and poked him on the chest and a loud majestic voice thundered, "Because you bug me, Kirk."

Ever felt that way? Ever felt as though God were saying to you, "You bug me"? If the truth were told, everyone of us has at one time or another felt that God was teed off at us. We have looked at the circumstances of our lives and felt that if God really cared, none of this would be happening to us.

In those times of difficulty, loneliness and despair, the church has too often responded with polite platitudes, empty epiphanies, callused cacophonies of spiritual drivel. Too often we have simply said, "Now, now; just trust God and everything will be all right." In doing so we have discounted the person and the hurt he or she bears. We have also reduced God to a nebulous entity that somehow, somewhere can be trusted. How and for what we just never get around to.

This reminds me of a third-grade teacher who asked her class to draw a picture of something that frightened them, something of which they were afraid. They had all finished their pictures, and she was going around the room looking at each of them and talking with each child about his fears. When she got to Johnny, she saw he had drawn a very large and frightening tornado coming toward a man standing outside his car. She said, "Oh, a tornado! I guess the man better pray, don't you Johnny?" "No," Johnny said, "I think he ought to run like hell!"

While I do not approve of Johnny's language, I must confess, I am sympathetic to his sentiments. There is a time to pray and a time to run.

FORM: *How will I say it?*

The primary form of this sermon is narrative in a significant portion.

Not long ago I returned to Wilmore, Kentucky, where I met my bride and where I went to school for three years. As I was driving into Lexington one night, I remembered a night more than 30 years ago. It was the night of the worst band of tornadoes to ever hit the US. Jane and I were at our little church in Eastern Kentucky. The service had ended that Wednesday night and we started the 65-mile drive back home, through Lexington and on to Wilmore. We were caught in the worst thunderstorm I have ever witnessed. Then we saw where a tornado had picked up farm equipment and trees and tossed them onto the expressway, just like in the movie, "Twister."

I turned on the radio and began to hear reports of the terrible damage done to Conyers, Georgia, and vast destruction through Tennessee, Kentucky and Ohio. Large sections of Xenia, Ohio, had been completely destroyed. As we drove through Lexington, no lights shone and the streets were eerily empty. As we left Lexington and started toward Wilmore, the announcer on the radio told us that a tornado was spotted near Harrodsburg and was headed toward Lexington. Wilmore is located directly between Harrodsburg and Lexington.

I didn't know what else to do, so I drove on to Wilmore and ran through the blinding rain and howling wind into the house. Jane and I immediately lighted a candle and knelt by the side of the bed to pray. As we prayed, the wind howled all around that little cinder-block apartment.

When we were more or less prayed out and as the wind kept howling and the lightning kept the night sky alight, I began to undress. Jane looked at me in horror and said, "What are you doing?" I said, "Jane, I am home. I don't have anywhere else to go. I have finished praying. There is nothing else I can do. I am going to go to sleep. If I am going to die tonight, it might as well be in my sleep."

I want to ask you to give me the benefit of the doubt. I had been a husband only for a year. I was not so sensitive and caring as I am today. Jane was not happy with my cavalier attitude toward what appeared to be imminent death. For some reason, she expected me to hold her and comfort her until the night had passed and the danger was over. I wanted to go to sleep. I know better, now! But I remember how young and stupid I was then.

When trouble comes, we want to know someone somewhere cares. But we especially want to know God cares. We want to know if we really can trust God. Does He know and does He care?

A little boy was standing on the sidewalk in the middle of a block. He was obviously waiting for something. An older man approached him and asked for what he was waiting. The little guy confidently told the older man that he was waiting for the bus. The man laughed and said the bus stop was in the next block. The boy acknowledged that fact but insisted the bus would stop for him right here. The older man became annoyed at what he thought was insolence. He raised his voice and told the boy that he had better start walking if he hoped to ride that bus. The boy politely turned down the suggestion and said he would wait for the bus where he stood. The man fumed at the little boy and started walking off. Before the man was too far away, he heard the screeching of brakes. He turned around and couldn't believe his eyes. The bus was actually stopping for the little boy. The bus door opened and the youngster started to board. Just before he did, he turned toward the man down the street and yelled, "My daddy is the bus driver!"

Now we know why the boy was so secure. He knew the bus driver. He had a relationship with the bus driver.

Now you know why I could go to sleep in the middle of the storm of the century. I knew the bus driver! He's my daddy! While that does not explain the insensitivity of a young husband to his worried wife, it does explain the peace God had and has given me.

It is a peace that passes understanding. It exists because I know God knows and God cares. I knew that night 28 years ago that if I survived, I could trust God. If I died, I would be in the bosom of my Father.

On a night on the Sea of Galilee almost 2,000 years ago a storm raged. The men in a boat were very frightened. Yet One slept in the bow of the boat oblivious to the storm surging around them. His name is Jesus. The frightened disciples woke him up and said, "Lord, don't you care?"

Have you ever been there? Have you ever been in the midst of the storm of your life and wondered, "Does Jesus care? Does God care?" Maybe you are there today. Maybe today a storm is raging in your life and you wonder whether God even cares. Perhaps you are in the midst of chemotherapy, or your husband just walked out on you, or your child is in serious trouble, or your finances are falling apart, or your parents are dying. Does God care? Listen to what Jesus said in Luke 12:6:

> "Are not five sparrows sold for two pennies? Yet not one of them is forgotten by God. Indeed, the very hairs of your head are all numbered. Don't be afraid; you are worth more than many sparrows."

Not a single sparrow is forgotten by God. Now what is worth less in the world's economy than a single sparrow? What is one sparrow, more or less? Does it make any difference to you if a sparrow flies into the windshield of a truck on I-75 in Cincinnati?

It matters to God. Yet Jesus is not teaching us here about how much God cares for a single sparrow. The teaching is much more important than that.

What Jesus is teaching us here is a lesson of comparison and contrast. Don't be afraid. You are worth more than many sparrows. Why, even the hairs on your head are numbered.

I get my hair cut every few weeks. The last time the stylist said,

"Oh, hair number 423 just fell out." I was devastated. I loved hair 423. It was right next to hair 424 for 50 years. Now it is gone. Another one bites the dust!

Now, that didn't really happen. I don't know how many hairs I have on my head. I know only that they are getting fewer and fewer. I certainly don't have each hair individually numbered. But God does.

Jesus tells us this to illustrate how very much God cares for us. He cares for us more than we even care for ourselves. He cares for us more than he cares for many sparrows—yet he cares for every sparrow.

John Wesley, the founder of the Methodist movement in England in the 18th century, was preaching on this text and said:

> "Are not ye much better than they? Shall he not then 'much more feed you,' who are pre-eminent by so much odds? He does not, in that sense, look upon you and them 'with equal eyes;' set you on a level with them . . . in respect of life and death: 'Right precious in the sight of the Lord is the death of his saints.' Do you really think the death of a sparrow is equally precious in his sight? He tells us, indeed, that 'not a sparrow falleth on the ground without our Father;' but he asks at the same time, 'Are ye not of more value than many sparrows?"[1]

My daddy never had much use for animals. When I was a boy, I had a dog, but he never had a dog. I inherited my disdain for cats from my father. He had no use for cats and no time for dogs. He was too busy making a living for his family.

I cannot tell you how surprised I was one day to get home from school and find a box sitting on the counter of our store. Inside was a little bird. It was so young it barely had feathers on it. It was jet black. It was a baby crow. Daddy had found that helpless bird when he was out delivering groceries. He carefully gathered it up, put it in a cardboard box on pine straw and brought it back to the store. He asked me if I wanted to take care of that helpless baby crow.

For days and weeks I fed and cared for that helpless bird until one day Daddy told me it was time to let it go. We turned it loose and it flew away.

What I will always remember is that Daddy rescued a helpless bird from the side of the road. This was a man who had no time for pets, but could not let something suffer if he could do anything about it. He saw that bird and had to help.

Just like my father saw the helpless bird, God sees and cares for you and me in our helplessness. And there is nothing for which we are more helpless than our spiritual condition. We are lost. We are spiritually dead. We are unable to do anything to save ourselves from the penalty and power of our sin.

Yet God in his infinite love and care for us intervenes for us. He rescues us from the roadside of hell and carries us in his own bosom, safe and secure in his grace.

How do I know? Two ways: First of all, the witness of the Word of God tells me the great story of the love of God for me and all of fallen humanity. It is the story of Jesus—his birth, his life, his death, and his resurrection. Secondly, I know because of the witness of his Spirit. I believed the gospel, and God has given to me the witness of the Spirit in my spirit that I am in fact a child of God.

I have found a secure place, I have found a place of caring, and I have found a place of comfort in the wonderful grace of Jesus. It is a place so secure that I can sleep in the midst of the storm. It is a place so real and so deep that when life has thrown its worst at me, I have known that God cares for me.

I am thankful that along life's way others have cared for me, many others. But, "No one ever cared for me like Jesus."

FUNCTION: *What is God is inviting us to do?*

The function of this sermon is to invite the worshiper to learn to trust in God's care for his or her life through the use of relevant Scripture verses.

Do you need to know that Jesus cares for you today? Are you experiencing trauma or distress? Do fear or anxiety poison your life? Do you need to know that Jesus cares for you?

I want to invite you to take the bookmark you received in your worship folder. Look at the side that lists some of the promises of God. Mark the ones that you need to claim in your own life. Then I invite you to take the bookmark home with you and each day memorize one of the promises of God. Learn it in the morning and repeat it as Dr. Pepper®—at 10, 2, and 4. Then share it with a friend, a child or a spouse before you go to bed at night. This week, live in the promises and assurance of God in Christ.

[1] Sermon 67 text; from 1872 edition On Divine Providence